ESSENTIAL SAROYAN

ESSENTIAL SAROYAN

Edited with an Introduction by
WILLIAM E. JUSTICE

Santa Clara University, Santa Clara, California
Heyday Books, Berkeley, California

Our gratitude to Robert Setrakian and the William Saroyan Foundation.

© 2005 by The Trustees of Leland Stanford Jr. University
Introduction © 2005 by William E. Justice

All rights reserved. No portion of this work may be reproduced or transmitted
in any form or by any means, electronic or mechanical, including photocopying
and recording, or by any information storage or retrieval system, without permission
in writing from Heyday Books.

Heyday Books, founded in 1974, works to deepen people's understanding and
appreciation of the cultural, artistic, historic, and natural resources of California
and the American West. It operates under a 501(c)(3) nonprofit educational
organization (Heyday Institute) and, in addition to publishing books, sponsors a wide
range of programs, outreach, and events.

To help support Heyday or to learn more about us, visit our website at
www.heydaybooks.com, or write to us at P.O. Box 9145, Berkeley, CA 94709.

Library of Congress Cataloging-in-Publication Data

Saroyan, William, 1908-
  [Selections. 2005]
  Essential Saroyan / edited by William E. Justice.
      p. cm. — (A California legacy book)
  "Major works by William Saroyan": p.
  ISBN 1-59714-001-5 (pbk. : alk. paper)
  1. California—Literary collections. I. Justice, William E. II.
  Title. III. Series.
  PS3537.A826A6 2005
  813'.52—dc22
                              2004028318

Cover Art and Design: Lorraine Rath
Interior Design/Typesetting: Philip Krayna, PKD, Berkeley
Printing and Binding: McNaughton & Gunn, Saline, MI

Orders, inquiries, and correspondence should be addressed to:
      Heyday Books
      P.O. Box 9145, Berkeley, CA 94709
      (510) 549-3564, Fax (510) 549-1889
      www.heydaybooks.com

Printed in the United States of America

10 9 8 7 6 5 4 3 2 1

Contents

Introduction

This book is a valentine. It is not an open valentine, but one that lurks; it sits on a shelf and it waits. Its pages swarm with life and joy, but not without the occasional sting. Between its innocent covers can be found cold watermelons, bicycles, stolen horses, cars, ripe pears, and tigers in a vast parade of locomotion and feasting. Its heroes are Assyrian, German, Japanese, American, and Armenian. But lest you take its sentiment lightly, be warned: it hides a landmine. It may leave you forever changed.

There are certain writers that find us in youth, or in a moment of youth when we're bent-backed and hoary, who cause a strange and irreversible reaction. Literary people are made this way, almost by accident, by stumbling into a writer, unsuspecting and unknowing, then...Boom! You are tossed in the air, limbs flailing and half-conscious, and when you land in a heap and start counting your fingers and toes, you notice something: you're no longer just a person. You have become a *literary* person. A writer, a critic, an enthusiast, a librarian, a diarist, an editor, a propagandist, a publisher, a journalist, or, God help you, a poet. Pick whichever you like, the transformation is the same, families are shamed, the landmine has done its indelible work.

William Saroyan is such a writer.

These human landmines are rare and essential parts of the literary world, but the distinction has its disadvantages. Adults are notorious for repudiating the tastes of their youth, and to the professional critic such authors are vexing. *Time* magazine wrote at the

end of Saroyan's career that "the ease and charm of many of his stories will continue to inspire young writers. It is a legacy beyond
criticism." Saroyan was plagued by rotten reviews his whole life,
and even when *Time* attempted a compliment, it was backhanded.
To be "beyond criticism" is not necessarily a good way to stay in
print. Once the most famous writer on earth, Saroyan is currently
little known to readers under forty, but he belongs in the company
of Kahlil Gibran, Dylan Thomas, J. D. Salinger, C. S. Lewis, the
Brontës, Dostoevsky, Jack Kerouac, Sylvia Plath, Heinrich Heine,
Madeleine L'Engle, and Arthur Conan Doyle; he belongs among
those writers who steal us from youth.

Fellow Armenian David Kherdian eulogized Saroyan as the
"poet of childhood," but that label just misses the mark. Saroyan is
the poet of *adolescence*. His is the genius of a youth suddenly noticing
the World and trying to swallow it whole. Saroyan is the poet of the
time when we know only childhood but we desire everything else.
This is the magic, longing, and ease of Saroyan's best work. It is what
makes him the immortal he always wanted to be.

Richard Rodriguez describes the phenomenon perfectly: "His
name was William Saroyan. He was the first writer I fell in love
with, boyishly in love. I was held by his unaffected voice, his
sentimentality, his defiant individualism. I found myself in the
stories he told."

That is Saroyan's legacy. The man is another kettle of fish entirely.

William Saroyan was born in Fresno, California, to Armenian
immigrants in 1908; the century we recently crawled out of
had only just begun. Henry Ford had just invented the Model T, the
first long-distance radio message was sent, the sun still hadn't set on
the English empire, and the first passenger flight skittered into the
air for a whole minute. Saroyan's father died when he was three and
little Willie was taken to an orphanage in Oakland. Five years later
his mother was able to bring her kids back. William hated the
orphanage with a passionate disinterest and tried to forget his years
there completely. It is only noteworthy in regards to Saroyan's work
in its absence. Saroyan's Armenian heritage, however, manifests

itself in his writing in a number of ways, perhaps most strikingly in
the novel *My Name is Aram,* hailed as "the Armenian *Huck Finn.*"
Saroyan found, and was found by, Armenians wherever he went
and quickly became a hero and a favorite son. Today, love of
Saroyan's writing is handed down from generation to generation
along with famous recipes and stories of their glorious past.

Back in Fresno, Saroyan proved to be an indifferent student, a
ravenous reader, and a reliable bike messenger. Fresno at the time
was an immigrant town, and Saroyan's classmates were German,
Chinese, Irish, Jewish, Japanese, Turkish, and a whole grab bag of
other recent immigrants that made lively if discordant noise of the
city streets. This unique California town would come to symbolize
the entire United States for Saroyan, and contribute to his steadfast
belief that countries, races, religions, and wars were all dross and
nonsense and that any politicians, generals, or businessmen who
said otherwise were crooks and scoundrels or worse. Moreover, he
believed not only that he could shame war and its supporters but
that he could cheat death. The sheer, unabashed *adolescence* of the
man, with all its bravado, sentiment, and defiant idealism, came to
define Saroyan. Even in his later writings, when they worked, Saroyan
sang with the same voice that he had first cultivated as a young man.

Saroyan found his own landmine writer when he was twelve,
during a visit to the Fresno Public Library. The author, buried
innocently among thousands of other books that would not have
done the trick, was Guy de Maupassant. Young Saroyan read with
rapt attention the story of a one-legged cripple nicknamed Bell for
the way his body swung between his crutches. Bell is chased from
home to home, not a bread crust in his belly, until he is finally
arrested and dies of hunger. At that moment, when Bell gave up the
ghost—kaboom!—William Saroyan, the writer, was born. One
year later he dropped out of high school in order to attend a technical school. The most important skill a writer could have, believed
young Saroyan, was the ability to type very, very fast. For the first
time in his life, he was a top student.

In 1934 America was harried and humbled by the Great
Depression, and Europe was already engaged in the insanity that led
to World War II. Saroyan, then twenty-six, undertook a brash and

presumptuous stunt. In a feat of sheer literary athleticism he wrote one short story a day for thirty days, mailing each one to *Story* magazine. A year later the collection, *The Daring Young Man on the Flying Trapeze,* was published. It became a best-seller, and Saroyan was famous. In true Saroyan style, he promptly took a trip around the world, writing stories and impressions at every stop. In the preface of that collection, he wrote:

> The most solid advice for a writer is this, I think: Try to learn to breathe deeply, really to taste food when you eat, and when you sleep really to sleep. Try as much as possible to be wholly alive with all your might, and when you laugh, laugh like hell. And when you get angry, get good and angry. Try to be alive. You will be dead soon enough.

That collection was followed up by several more, and Saroyan's sudden fame increased.

This would prove to be a charmed time for Saroyan. In six short years he'd written several best-selling collections of short stories and two Broadway hits, traveled the globe, and even worked in Hollywood, though with strained and unsatisfying results. Owing to an intervening world war, a wildly unsuccessful marriage, and the steady march into middle age, Saroyan, though he continued to publish until the end of his life, would never recapture the ease and pleasure of those years.

Saroyan's Fresno youth had been a golden time. Though hardly a pampered existence, his life had been filled with adventure and drama. He was surrounded by immigrants, farmers, laborers, small businessmen, and bums, and he moved among them, delivering telegrams or selling papers, almost as an equal. It was the strength and hidden nobility of these people that piqued Saroyan's curiosity and became the material for his best work. In contrast, the life of a celebrity surrounded by other celebrities, moguls, and critics, moving from Paris to London to New York to San Francisco as the mood took him, failed to make him happy and provided little material worth writing about. There is a lesson there for young writers.

The depressing times that follow will go quickly. In 1942, at thirty-four, he was drafted into the United States Army and married a teenaged New York debutante. Although World War II is now commonly thought of as the "good war," Saroyan went bitterly. His friend and fellow writer John Steinbeck offered to pull some strings for him so he could stay out of the war, but, strangely, Saroyan declined. He didn't see combat but was shipped off to London and stayed there during the bombardment, by that time leaving behind not only a young wife but also a son, Aram.

When the army asked Saroyan to write a cheering story of the American soldier in London, Saroyan created Wesley Jackson, who did not want to be a soldier at all and whose primary response to the war was fear:

> The minute a War starts everybody seems to forget everything he ever knew—everything that's worth a hoot—and shuts his mouth and keeps it shut and just groans with agony about the lies he hears all over the place all the time.

The Army was not amused by the overall tone of the novel and suppressed it. *The Adventures of Wesley Jackson* was not published until after the war was over.

For Saroyan, the army was another orphanage. His movements were controlled, he was separated from his loved ones, and his inherent singularity was despised and ignored. Aside from *The Adventures of Wesley Jackson,* Saroyan didn't write at all during his enlistment and was discharged a bitter, broken man.

Furthermore, his marriage was falling apart, despite the birth of another child, this time a daughter. Both parents were probably to blame. Saroyan was moody, jealous, and irresponsible. His wife, Carol, was young, spoiled, and ambitious. Before, during, and after her marriage to Saroyan she was courted by, among others, Orson Welles, Clifford Odets, Al Capp (creator of "Lil' Abner"), and Marlon Brando (who later dallied with Lucy, Saroyan's daughter) before finally marrying Walter Matthau, after divorcing Saroyan not once but twice. These rarefied dramas were a far cry from the life of plucky immigrants in Fresno, and they ill-suited Saroyan. It was a tumultuous and ugly time that resurfaced whenever he saw his children; Saroyan's feelings toward them vacillated between total adoration and repulsion.

Though he went on to write some of his best work after 1945, including "Tracy's Tiger," Saroyan never recovered from his service in World War II or his failed marriage. His writing became more and more self-referential, even to the point of publishing journals and travel diaries, and the quality varied greatly. Although some of the writing is as lucid and moving as his early work, it is clear that many of his books were rushed through in order to pay off his gambling debts: he was known to lose as much as sixty thousand dollars in a single day.

Saroyan, whose career began with a literary stunt, ended it with another. From his final hospital bed he sent a statement out on the AP wire: "Everybody has got to die, but I always believed an exception would be made in my case. Now what?"

He died in May of 1981. Ronald Reagan was president, the *Columbia* space shuttle had its first successful launch, and Pac-Man was taking the country's youth by storm. The world he grew up in and wrote so touchingly about was all but forgotten. After his death, half of his ashes were sent to Fresno, California, and the other half to Yerevan, Armenia, to be enshrined in the Pantheon of Greats.

As a writer, Saroyan was an athlete. His stories often feel like the work of a grand acrobat or a daredevil escapist. His prose is not studied. His plots are not intricate. His stories are not proper stories. They ramble, exclaim, and take strange detours. In many ways, they resemble dice games, with sudden turns of luck and surprising, even unlikely, combinations of events and characters. His plays, too, are strange and unconventional creatures, including *The Time of Your Life,* for which he won a Pulitzer Prize in 1940. These traits do not make him a difficult writer, however. In fact, few can be read so easily.

Saroyan invented his very own style, without shaping or molding by universities, and brought an unerring sense of life to the written word that beguiles and captivates. For this alone, that he wrote stunningly in a voice wholly his own and without precedent, he should be admired and studied. The literary world today could use more of his brash intensity, experimentalism, and intolerance of compromise.

Saroyan set out to challenge the world. He felt proud, untamable strength in his writing and muscled his way into literature. To read him is to feel an almost physical exuberance.

We need writers who refuse to grow up. Who else will ensnare unsuspecting youths and transform them? How else will we keep this literary world going? Some of the more tiresome adults, many critics among them, believe they have no further use for *adolescence,* but they are mistaken. For though Saroyan's defiance may be immature, and though his ambitions childish, his angry questions to the world remain unanswered. No one else is even asking them. Saroyan was always aware that his concerns would be ignored by certain people, and answered them thus:

> I'm asking for sophisticated people to laugh. That is what sophistication is for. I do not believe in races. I do not believe in governments. I see life as one at a time, so many millions simultaneously all over the earth. Babies who have not yet been taught to speak any language are the only race of the earth, the race of man: all else is pretence, what we call civilization, hatred, fear, desire for strength....But a baby is a baby. And the way they cry, there you have the brotherhood of man, babies crying.

And now, without further ado, high above the ring to my right, *he flies through the air with the greatest of ease...*

The Daring Young Man on the Flying Trapeze

CHAPTER 1 *Sleep*

Horizontally wakeful amid universal widths, practicing laughter and mirth, satire, the end of all, Rome and yes of Babylon, clenched teeth, remembrance, much warmth volcanic, the streets of Paris, the plains of Jericho, much gliding as of reptile in abstraction, a gallery of watercolors, the sea and the fish with eyes, symphony, a table in the corner of the Eiffel Tower, jazz at the opera house, alarm clock and the tapdancing of doom, conversation with a tree, the river Nile, the roar of Dostoevsky, and the dark sun.

This earth, the face of one who lived, the form without the weight, weeping upon snow, white music, the magnified flower twice the size of the universe, black clouds, the caged panther staring, deathless space, Mr. Eliot with rolled sleeves baking bread, Flaubert and Guy de Maupassant, a wordless rhyme of early meaning, Finlandia, mathematics highly polished and slick as a green onion to the teeth, Jerusalem, the path to paradox.

The deep song of man, the sly whisper of someone unseen but vaguely known, hurricane in the cornfield, a game of chess, hush the queen, the king, Karl Franz, black Titanic, Mr. Chaplin weeping, Stalin, Hitler, a multitude of Jews, tomorrow is Monday, no dancing in the streets.

O swift moment of life: it is ended, again the earth is now.

CHAPTER 2 *Wakefulness*

He (the living) dressed and shaved, grinning at himself in the mirror. Very unhandsome, he said; where is my tie? (He had but one.) Coffee and a grey sky, Pacific Ocean fog, the drone of a passing street car, people going to the city, time again, the day, prose and poetry. He moved swiftly down the stairs to the street and began to walk, thinking suddenly. *It is only in sleep that we may know we live. There only, in that living death, do we meet ourselves and the far earth, God and the saints, the names of our fathers, the substance of remote moments: it is there that the centuries merge in the moment, that the vast becomes the tiny, tangible atom of eternity.*

He walked into the day as alertly as might be, making a definite noise with his heels, perceiving with his eyes the superficial truth of streets and structures, the trivial truth of reality. Helplessly his mind sang, *He flies through the air with the greatest of ease, the daring young man on the flying trapeze,* then laughed with all the might of his being. It was really a splendid morning—grey, cold, and cheerless, a morning for inward vigor; ah, Edgar Guest, he said, how I long for your music.

In the gutter he saw a coin which proved to be a penny dated 1923, and placing it in the palm of his hand he examined it closely, remembering that year and thinking of Lincoln, whose profile was stamped upon the coin. There was almost nothing a man could do with a penny. I will purchase a motor-car, he thought. I will dress myself in the fashion of a fop, visit the hotel strumpets, drink and dine, and then return to the quiet. Or I will drop the coin into a slot and weigh myself.

It was good to be poor, and the Communists—but it was dreadful to be hungry. What appetites they had, how fond they were of food! Empty stomachs. He remembered how greatly he needed food. Every meal was bread and coffee and cigarettes, and now he had no more bread. Coffee without bread could never honestly serve as supper, and there were no weeds in the park that could be cooked as spinach is cooked.

If the truth were known he was half starved, and there was still no end of books he ought to read before he died. He remembered the young Italian in a Brooklyn hospital, a small sick clerk named Mollica, who had said desperately, I would like to see California once before I die. And he thought earnestly, I ought at least to read *Hamlet* once again; or perhaps *Huckleberry Finn*.

It was then that he became thoroughly awake: at the thought of dying. Now wakefulness was a state in the nature of a sustained shock. A young man could perish rather unostentatiously, he thought; and already he was very nearly starved. Water and prose were fine, they filled much inorganic space, but they were inadequate. If there were only some work he might do for money, some trivial labor in the name of commerce. If they would only allow him to sit at a desk all day and add trade figures, subtract and multiply and divide, then perhaps he would not die. He would buy food, all sorts of it: untasted delicacies from Norway, Italy, and France; all manner of beef, lamb, fish, cheese, grapes, figs, pears, apples, melons, which he would worship when he had satisfied his hunger. He would place a bunch of red grapes on a dish beside two black figs, a large yellow pear, and a green apple. He would hold a cut melon to his nostrils for hours. He would buy great brown loaves of French bread, vegetables of all sorts, meat, life.

From a hill he saw the city standing majestically in the east, great towers, dense with his kind, and there he was suddenly outside of it all, almost definitely certain that he should never gain admittance, almost positive that somehow he had ventured upon the wrong earth, or perhaps into the wrong age, and now a young man of twenty-two was to be permanently ejected from it. This thought was not saddening. He said to himself, sometime soon I must write *An Application for Permission to Live*. He accepted the thought of dying without pity for himself or for man, believing that he would at least sleep another night. His rent for another day was paid; there was yet another tomorrow. And after that he might go where other homeless men went. He might even visit the Salvation Army—sing to God and Jesus (unlover of my soul), be saved, eat and sleep. But he knew that he would not. His life was a private life. He did not wish to destroy this fact. Any other alternative would be better.

Through the air on the flying trapeze, his mind hummed. Amusing it was, astoundingly funny. A trapeze to God, or to nothing, a flying trapeze to some sort of eternity; he prayed objectively for strength to make the flight with grace.

I have one cent, he said. It is an American coin. In the evening I shall polish it until it glows like a sun and I shall study the words.

He was now walking in the city itself, among living men. There were one or two places to go. He saw his reflection in plate-glass windows of stores and was disappointed with his appearance. He seemed not at all as strong as he felt; he seemed, in fact, a trifle infirm in every part of his body, in his neck, his shoulders, arms, trunk, and knees. This will never do, he said, and with an effort he assembled all his disjointed parts and became tensely, artificially erect and solid.

He passed numerous restaurants with magnificent discipline, refusing even to glance into them, and at last reached a building which he entered. He rose in an elevator to the seventh floor, moved down a hall, and, opening a door, walked into the office of an employment agency. Already there were two dozen young men in the place; he found a corner where he stood waiting his turn to be interviewed. At length he was granted this great privilege and was questioned by a thin, scatter-brained miss of fifty.

Now tell me, she said; what can you do?

He was embarrassed. I can write, he said pathetically.

You mean your penmanship is good? Is that it? said the elderly maiden.

Well, yes, he replied. But I mean that I can write.

Write what? said the miss, almost with anger.

Prose, he said simply.

There was a pause. At last the lady said:

Can you use a typewriter?

Of course, said the young man.

All right, went on the miss, we have your address; we will get in touch with you. There is nothing this morning, nothing at all.

It was much the same at the other agency, except that he was questioned by a conceited young man who closely resembled a pig. From the agencies he went to the large department stores: there was a good deal of pomposity, some humiliation on his part, and finally the report that work was not available. He did not feel displeased, and strangely did not even feel that he was personally involved in all the foolishness. He was a living young man who was in need of money with which to go on being one, and there was no way of getting it except by working for it; and there was no work. It was purely an abstract problem which he wished for the last time to attempt to solve. Now he was pleased that the matter was closed.

He began to perceive the definiteness of the course of his life. Except for moments, it had been largely artless, but now at the last minute he was determined that there should be as little imprecision as possible.

He passed countless stores and restaurants on his way to the Y.M.C.A., where he helped himself to paper and ink and began to compose his *Application*. For an hour he worked on this document, then suddenly, owing to the bad air in the place and to hunger, he became faint. He seemed to be swimming away from himself with great strokes, and hurriedly left the building. In the Civic Center Park, across from the Public Library Building, he drank almost a quart of water and felt himself refreshed. An old man was standing in the center of the brick boulevard surrounded by sea-gulls, pigeons, and robins. He was taking handfuls of bread crumbs from a large paper sack and tossing them to the birds with a gallant gesture.

Dimly he felt impelled to ask the old man for a portion of the crumbs, but would not allow the thought even nearly to reach consciousness; he entered the Public Library and for an hour read Proust, then, feeling himself to be swimming away again, he rushed outdoors. He drank more water at the fountain in the park and began the long walk to his room.

I'll go and sleep some more, he said; there is nothing else to do. He knew now that he was much too tired and weak to deceive himself about being all right, and yet his mind seemed somehow still lithe and alert. It, as if it were a separate entity, persisted in articulating impertinent pleasantries about his very real physical suffering. He reached his room early in the afternoon and immediately prepared coffee on the small gas range. There was no milk in the can, and the half pound of sugar he had purchased a week before was all gone; he drank a cup of the hot black fluid, sitting on his bed and smiling.

From the Y.M.C.A. he had stolen a dozen sheets of letter paper upon which he hoped to complete his document, but now the very notion of writing was unpleasant to him. There was nothing to say. He began to polish the penny he had found in the morning, and this absurd act somehow afforded him great enjoyment. No American coin can be made to shine so brilliantly as a penny. How many pennies would he need to go on living? Wasn't there something more he might sell? He looked about the bare room. No. His watch was gone, also his books. All those fine books; nine of them for eighty-five cents. He felt ill and ashamed for having parted with his books. His best suit he had sold for two dollars, but that was all right. He didn't mind at all about clothes. But the books. That was different. It made him very angry to think that there was no respect for men who wrote.

He placed the shining penny on the table, looking upon it with the delight of a miser. How prettily it smiles, he said. Without reading them he looked at the words, *E Pluribus Unum One Cent United States of America,* and turning the penny over, he saw Lincoln and the words *In God We Trust Liberty* 1923. How beautiful it is, he said.

He became drowsy and felt a ghastly illness coming over his blood, a feeling of nausea and disintegration. Bewildered, he stood beside his bed, thinking *there is nothing to do but sleep.* Already he felt himself making great strides through the fluid of the earth, swimming away to the beginning. He fell face down upon the bed, saying, I ought first at least to give the coin to some child. A child could buy any number of things with a penny.

Then swiftly, neatly, with the grace of the young man on the trapeze, he was gone from his body. For an eternal moment he was all things at once: the bird, the fish, the rodent, the reptile, and man. An ocean of print undulated endlessly and darkly before him. The city burned. The herded crowd rioted. The earth circled away, and knowing that he did so, he turned his lost face to the empty sky and became dreamless, unalive, perfect.

Seventy Thousand Assyrians

I hadn't had a haircut in forty days and forty nights, and I was beginning to look like several violinists out of work. You know the look: genius gone to pot, and ready to join the Communist Party. We barbarians from Asia Minor are hairy people: when we need a haircut, we *need* a haircut. It was so bad, I had outgrown my only hat. (I am writing a serious story, perhaps one of the most serious I shall ever write. That is why I am being flippant. Readers of Sherwood Anderson will begin to understand what I am saying after a while; they will know that my laughter is rather sad.) I was a young man in need of a haircut, so I went down to Third Street (San Francisco), to the Barber College, for a fifteen-cent haircut.

Third Street, below Howard, is a district; think of the Bowery in New York, Main Street in Los Angeles: think of old men and boys, out of work, hanging around, smoking Bull Durham, talking about the government, waiting for something to turn up, simply waiting. It was a Monday morning in August and a lot of the tramps had come to the shop to brighten up a bit. The Japanese boy who was working over the free chair had a waiting list of eleven; all the other chairs were occupied. I sat down and began to wait. Outside, as Hemingway (*The Sun Also Rises, A Farewell to Arms, Death in the Afternoon, Winner Take Nothing*) would say, haircuts were four bits. I had twenty cents and a half pack of Bull Durham. I rolled a cigarette, handed the pack to one of my contemporaries who looked in need of nicotine, and inhaled the dry smoke, thinking of America, what was going on politically, economically, spiritually. My contemporary was a boy of sixteen. He looked Iowa; splendid potentially, a solid American, but down, greatly down in the mouth. Little sleep, no change of clothes for several days, a little fear, etc. I

wanted very much to know his name. A writer is always wanting to
get the reality of faces and figures. Iowa said, 'I just got in from
Salinas. No work in the lettuce fields. Going north now, to Portland;
try to ship out.' I wanted to tell him how it was with me: rejected
story from *Scribner's*, rejected essay from *The Yale Review*, no money
for decent cigarettes, worn shoes, old shirts, but I was afraid to make
something of my own troubles. A writer's troubles are always boring,
a bit unreal. People are apt to feel, *Well, who asked you to write in the
first place?* A man must pretend not to be a writer. I said, 'Good luck,
north.' Iowa shook his head. 'I know better. Give it a try, anyway.
Nothing to lose.' Fine boy, hope he isn't dead, hope he hasn't frozen,
mighty cold these days (December, 1933), hope he hasn't gone down;
he deserved to live. Iowa, I hope you got work in Portland; I hope
you are earning money; I hope you have rented a clean room with
a warm bed in it; I hope you are sleeping nights, eating regularly,
walking along like a human being, being happy. Iowa, my good
wishes are with you. I have said a number of prayers for you. (All
the same, I think he is dead by this time. It was in him the day I saw
him, the low malicious face of the beast, and at the same time all the
theaters in America were showing, over and over again, an animat-
ed film-cartoon in which there was a song called 'Who's Afraid of
the Big Bad Wolf?' and that's what it amounts to: people with
money laughing at the death that is crawling slyly into boys like
young Iowa, pretending that it isn't there, laughing in warm theaters. I have prayed for Iowa, and I consider myself a coward. By this
time he must be dead, and I am sitting in a small room, talking
about him, only talking.)

   I began to watch the Japanese boy who was learning to become a
barber. He was shaving an old tramp who had a horrible face, one
of those faces that emerge from years and years of evasive living,
years of being unsettled, of not belonging anywhere, of owning
nothing, and the Japanese boy was holding his nose back (his own
nose), so that he would not smell the old tramp. A trivial point in a
story, a bit of data with no place in a work of art, nevertheless, I put
it down. A young writer is always afraid some significant fact may
escape him. He is always wanting to put in everything he sees.
I wanted to know the name of the Japanese boy. I am profoundly

interested in names. I have found that those that are unknown are the most genuine. Take a big name like Andrew Mellon. I was watching the Japanese boy very closely. I wanted to understand from the way he was keeping his sense of smell away from the mouth and nostrils of the old man what he was thinking, how he was feeling. Years ago, when I was seventeen, I pruned vines in my uncle's vineyard, north of Sanger, in the San Joaquin Valley, and there were several Japanese working with me, Yoshio Enomoto, Hideo Suzuki, Katsumi Sujimoto, and one or two others. These Japanese taught me a few simple phrases, *hello, how are you, fine day, isn't it, good-bye,* and so on. I said in Japanese to the barber student, "How are you?" He said in Japanese, "Very well, thank you." Then, in impeccable English, "Do you speak Japanese? Have you lived in Japan?" I said, "Unfortunately, no. I am able to speak only one or two words. I used to work with Yoshio Enomoto, Hideo Suzuki, Katsumi Sujimoto; do you know them?" He went on with his work, thinking of the names. He seemed to be whispering, "Enomoto, Suzuki, Sujimoto." He said, "Suzuki. Small man?" I said, "Yes." He said, "I know him. He lives in San Jose now. He is married now."

I want you to know that I am deeply interested in what people remember. A young writer goes out to places and talks to people. He tries to find out what they remember. I am not using great material for a short story. Nothing is going to happen in this work. I am not fabricating a fancy plot. I am not creating memorable characters. I am not using a slick style of writing. I am not building up a fine atmosphere. I have no desire to sell this story or any story to *The Saturday Evening Post* or to *Cosmopolitan* or to *Harper's.* I am not trying to compete with the great writers of short stories, men like Sinclair Lewis and Joseph Hergesheimer and Zane Grey, men who really know how to write, how to make up stories that will sell. Rich men, men who understand all the rules about plot and character and style and atmosphere and all that stuff. I have no desire for fame. I am not out to win the Pulitzer Prize or the Nobel Prize or any other prize. I am out here in the far West, in San Francisco, in a small room on Carl Street, writing a letter to common people, telling them in simple language things they already know. I am merely making a record, so if I wander around a little, it is because I am in no hurry and because I do not know the rules. If I have any desire at all, it is to show the brotherhood of man. This is a big statement and it sounds a little precious. Generally a man is ashamed to make such a statement. He is afraid sophisticated people will laugh at him. But I don't mind. I'm asking sophisticated people to laugh. That is what sophistication is for. I do not believe in races. I do not believe in governments. I see life as one life at one time, so many millions simultaneously all over the earth. Babies who have not yet been taught to speak any language are the only race of the earth, the race of man: all the rest is pretence, what we call civilization, hatred, fear, desire for strength....But a baby is a baby. And the way they cry, there you have the brotherhood of man, babies crying. We grow up and we learn the words of a language and we see the universe through the language we know, we do not see it through all languages or through no language at all, through silence, for example, and we isolate ourselves in the language we know. Over here we isolate ourselves in English, or American as Mencken calls it. All the eternal things, in our words. If I want to do anything, I want to speak a more universal language. The heart of man, the unwritten part of man, that which is eternal and common to all races.

Now I am beginning to feel guilty and incompetent. I have used all this language and I am beginning to feel that I have said nothing. This is what drives a young writer out of his head, this feeling that nothing is being said. Any ordinary journalist would have been able to put the whole business into a three-word caption. Man is man, he would have said. Something clever, with any number of implications. But I want to use language that will create a single implication. I want the meaning to be precise, and perhaps that is why the language is so imprecise. I am walking around my subject, the impression I want to make, and I am trying to see it from all angles, so that I will have a whole picture, a picture of wholeness. It is the heart of man that I am trying to imply in this work.

Let me try again: I hadn't had a haircut in a long time and I was beginning to look seedy, so I went down to the Barber College on Third Street, and I sat in a chair. I said, "Leave it full in the back. I have a narrow head and if you do not leave it full in the back, I will go out of this place looking like a horse. Take as much as you like off the top. No lotion, no water, comb it dry." Reading makes a full man, writing a precise one, as you see. This is what happened. It doesn't make much of a story, and the reason is that I have left out the barber, the young man who gave me the haircut.

He was tall, he had a dark serious face, thick lips, on the verge of smiling but melancholy, thick lashes, sad eyes, a large nose. I saw his name on the card that was pasted on the mirror, Theodore Badal. A good name, genuine, a good young man, genuine. Theodore Badal began to work on my head. A good barber never speaks until he has been spoken to, no matter how full his heart may be.

"That name," I said, "Badal. Are you an Armenian?" I am an Armenian. I have mentioned this before. People look at me and begin to wonder, so I come right out and tell them, "I am an Armenian," I say. Or they read something I have written and begin to wonder, so I let them know. "I am an Armenian," I say. It is a meaningless remark, but they expect me to say it, so I do. I have no idea what it is like to be an Armenian or what it is like to be an Englishman or a Japanese or anything else. I have a faint idea what it is like to be alive. This is the only thing that interests me greatly. This and tennis. I hope some day to write a great philosophical work on tennis, something of the order of *Death in the Afternoon,* but I am aware that I am not yet ready to undertake such a work. I feel that the cultivation of tennis on a large scale among the peoples of the earth will do much to annihilate racial differences, prejudices, hatred, etc. Just as soon as I have perfected my drive and my lob, I hope to begin my outline of this great work. (It may seem to some sophisticated people that I am trying to make fun of Hemingway. I am not. *Death in the Afternoon* is a pretty sound piece of prose. I could never object to it as prose. I cannot even object to it as philosophy. I think it is finer philosophy than that of Will Durant and Walter Pitkin. Even when Hemingway is a fool, he is at least an accurate fool. He tells you what actually takes place and he doesn't allow the speed of an occurrence to make his exposition of it hasty. This is a lot. It is some sort of advancement for literature. To relate leisurely the nature and meaning of that which is very brief in duration.)

"Are you an Armenian?" I asked.

We are a small people and whenever one of us meets another, it is an event. We are always looking around for someone to talk to in our language. Our most ambitious political party estimates that there are nearly two million of us living on the earth, but most of us don't think so. Most of us sit down and take a pencil and a piece of paper and we take one section of the world at a time and imagine how many Armenians at the most are likely to be living in that section and we put the highest number on the paper, and then we go on to another section, India, Russia, Soviet Armenia, Egypt, Italy, Germany, France, America, South America, Australia, and so on, and after we add up our most hopeful figures the total comes to something a little less than a million. Then we start to think how big our families are, how high our birthrate and how low our deathrate (except in times of war when massacres increase the deathrate), and we begin to imagine how rapidly we will increase if we are left alone a quarter of a century, and we feel pretty happy. We always leave out earthquakes, wars, massacres, famines, etc., and it is a mistake. I remember the Near East Relief drives in my home town. My uncle used to be our orator and he used to make a whole auditorium full of Armenians weep. He was an attorney and he was a great orator. Well, at first the trouble was war. Our people were being destroyed by the enemy. Those who hadn't been killed were homeless and they were starving, *our own flesh and blood,* my uncle said, and we all wept. And we gathered money and sent it to our people in the old country. Then after the war, when I was a bigger boy, we had another Near East Relief drive and my uncle stood on the stage of the Civic Auditorium of my home town and he said, "Thank God this time it is not the enemy, but an earthquake. God has made us suffer. We have worshipped Him through trial and tribulation, through suffering and disease and torture and horror and (my uncle began to weep, began to sob) through the madness of despair, and now He has done this thing, and still we praise Him, still we worship Him. We do not understand the ways of God! And after the drive I went to my uncle and I said, "Did you mean what you said about God?" And he said, "That was oratory. We've got to raise money. What God? It is nonsense." "And when you cried?" I asked, and my uncle said, "That was real. I could not help it. I had to cry. Why, for God's sake, why must we go through all this God damn hell? What have we done to deserve all this torture? Man won't let us alone. God won't let us alone. Have we done something?

Aren't we supposed to be pious people? What is our sin? I am disgusted with God. I am sick of man. The only reason I am willing to get up and talk is that I don't dare keep my mouth shut. I can't bear the thought of more of our people dying. Jesus Christ, have we done something?"

I asked Theodore Badal if he was an Armenian.

He said, "I am an Assyrian."

Well, it was something. They, the Assyrians, came from our part of the world, they had noses like our noses, eyes like our eyes, hearts like our hearts. They had a different language. When they spoke we couldn't understand them, but they were a lot like us. It wasn't quite as pleasing as it would have been if Badal had been an Armenian, but it was something.

"I am an Armenian," I said, "I used to know some Assyrian boys in my home town, Joseph Sargis, Nito Elia, Tony Saleh. Do you know any of them?"

"Joseph Sargis, I know him," said Badal. "The others I do not know. We lived in New York until five years ago, then we came out west to Turlock. Then we moved up to San Francisco."

"Nito Elia," I said, "is a Captain in the Salvation Army." (I don't want anyone to imagine that I am making anything up, or that I am trying to be funny.) "Tony Saleh," I said, "was killed eight years ago. He was riding a horse and he was thrown and the horse began to run. Tony couldn't get himself free, he was caught by a leg, and the horse ran around and around for a half-hour and then stopped, and when they went up to Tony he was dead. He was fourteen at the time. I used to go to school with him. Tony was a very clever boy, very good at arithmetic."

We began to talk about the Assyrian language and the Armenian language, about the old world, conditions over there, and so on. I was getting a fifteen-cent haircut and I was doing my best to learn something at the same time, to acquire some new truth, some new appreciation of the wonder of life, the dignity of man. (Man has great dignity, do not imagine that he has not.)

Badal said, "I cannot read Assyrian. I was born in the old country, but I want to get over it."

He sounded tired, not physically but spiritually.

"Why?" I said. "Why do you want to get over it?"

"Well," he laughed, "simply because everything is washed up over there." I am repeating his words precisely, putting in nothing of my own. "We were a great people once," he went on. "But that was yesterday, the day before yesterday. Now we are a topic in ancient history. We had a great civilization. They're still admiring it. Now I am in America learning to cut hair. We're washed up as a race, we're through, it's all over, why should I learn to read the language? We have no writers, we have no news—well, there is a little news: once in a while the English encourage the Arabs to massacre us, that is all. It's an old story, we know all about it. The news comes over to us through the Associated Press, anyway."

These remarks were painful to me, an Armenian. I had always felt badly about my own people being destroyed. I had never heard an Assyrian speaking in English about such things. I felt great love for this young fellow. Don't get me wrong. There is a tendency these days to think in terms of pansies whenever a man says that he has affection for man. I think now that I have affection for all people, even for the enemies of Armenia, whom I have so tactfully not named. Everyone knows who they are. I have nothing against any of them because I think of them as one man living one life at a time, and I know, I am positive, that one man at a time is incapable of the monstrosities performed by mobs. My objection is to mobs only.

"Well," I said, "it is much the same with us. We, too, are old. We still have our church. We still have a few writers, Aharonian, Isahakian, a few others, but it is much the same."

"Yes," said the barber, "I know. We went in for the wrong things. We went in for the simple things, peace and quiet and families. We didn't go in for machinery and conquest and militarism. We didn't go in for diplomacy and deceit and the invention of machine-guns and poison gases. Well, there is no use being disappointed. We had our day, I suppose."

"We are hopeful," I said. "There is no Armenian living who does not still dream of an independent Armenia."

"Dream?" said Badal. "Well, that is something. Assyrians cannot even dream any more. Why, do you know how many of us are left on earth?"

"Two or three million," I suggested.

"Seventy thousand," said Badal. "That is all. Seventy thousand Assyrians in the world, and the Arabs are still killing us. They killed seventy of us in a little uprising last month. There was a small paragraph in the paper. Seventy more of us destroyed. We'll be wiped out before long. My brother is married to an American girl and he has a son. There is no more hope. We are trying to forget Assyria. My father still reads a paper that comes from New York, but he is an old man. He will be dead soon."

Then his voice changed, he ceased speaking as an Assyrian and began to speak as a barber: "Have I taken enough off the top?" he asked.

The rest of the story is pointless. I said *so long* to the young Assyrian and left the shop. I walked across town, four miles, to my room on Carl Street. I thought about the whole business: Assyria and this Assyrian, Theodore Badal, learning to be a barber, the sadness of his voice, the hopelessness of his attitude. This was months ago, in August, but ever since I have been thinking about Assyria, and I have been wanting to say something about Theodore Badal, a son of an ancient race, himself youthful and alert, yet hopeless. Seventy thousand Assyrians, a mere seventy thousand of that great people, and all the others quiet in death and all the greatness crumbled and ignored, and a young man in America learning to be a barber, and a young man lamenting bitterly the course of history.

Why don't I make up plots and write beautiful love stories that can be made into motion pictures? Why don't I let these unimportant and boring matters go hang? Why don't I try to please the American reading public?

Well, I am an Armenian. Michael Arlen is an Armenian, too. He is pleasing the public. I have great admiration for him, and I think he has perfected a very fine style of writing and all that, but I don't want to write about the people he likes to write about. Those people were dead to begin with. You take Iowa and the Japanese boy and Theodore Badal, the Assyrian; well, they may go down physically, like Iowa, to death, or spiritually, like Badal, to death, but they are of the stuff that is eternal in man and it is this stuff that interests me. You don't find them in bright places, making witty remarks about sex and trivial remarks about art. You find them where I found them. And they will be there forever, the race of man, the part of man, of Assyria as much as of England, that cannot be destroyed, the part that earthquake and war and famine and madness and everything else cannot destroy.

This work is in tribute to Iowa, to Japan, to Assyria, to Armenia, to the race of man everywhere, to the dignity of that race, the brotherhood of things alive. I am not expecting Paramount Pictures to film this work. I am thinking of seventy thousand Assyrians, one at a time, alive, a great race. I am thinking of Theodore Badal, himself seventy thousand Assyrians and seventy million Assyrians, himself Assyria, and man, standing in a barber's shop, in San Francisco, in 1933, and being, still, himself, the whole race.

Five Ripe Pears

If old man Pollard is still alive I hope he reads this because I want him to know I am not a thief and never have been. Instead of making up a lie, which I could have done, I told the truth, and got a licking. I don't care about the licking because I got a lot of them in grammar school. It was part of my education. Some of them I deserved, and some I didn't. The licking Mr. Pollard gave me I didn't deserve, and I hope he reads this because I am going to tell him why. I couldn't tell him that day because I didn't know how to explain what I knew. I am glad I haven't forgotten, though, because it is pretty important.

It was about spring pears.

The tree grew in a yard protected by a spike fence, but some of the branches grew beyond the fence. I was six, but a logician. A fence, I reasoned, can protect only that which it encloses.

Therefore, I said, the pears growing on the branches beyond the fence are mine—if I can reach them.

And I couldn't. Love of pears, though, encouraged the effort. I could see the pears, and I knew I wanted them. I did not want them only for eating, which would have been barbaric. I wanted them mostly for wanting them. I wanted pears, these being the closest at the time and most desirable. More, though, I wanted wanting and getting, and I invented means.

It was during school recess, and the trees were two blocks from school. I was thirsty for the sweet fluids of growing fruit, and for things less tangible. It is not stealing, I said.

It was adventure. Also art. Also religion, this sort of theft being a form of adoration. And it was exploration.

I told the Hebrew boy, Isaacs, I was going to the trees, and he said
it was stealing. This meant nothing, or it meant that he was afraid
to go with me. I did not bother at the time to investigate what it
meant, and went running out of the school grounds, down the
street. Peralta, I think it was. In minutes I did not know how long
recess endured, but I knew it never endured long. Certainly never
long *enough*. Recess should endure forever, was my opinion.

Running to pears as a boy of six is any number of classically
beautiful things: music and poetry and maybe war. I reached the
trees breathless but alert and smiling. The pears were fat and ready
for eating, and for plucking from limbs. They were ready. The sun
was warm. The moment was a moment of numerous clarities, air,
body, and mind.

Among the leaves I saw the pears, fat and yellow and red, full of it,
the stuff of life, from the sun, and I wanted. It was a thing they could
not speak about in the second grade because they hadn't found words
for it yet. They spoke only of the easiest things, but pears were basic
and not easy to speak of except as pears. If they spoke of pears at all
they would speak of them only as pears, so much a dozen, not as
shapes of living substance, miraculously; strange, exciting, and mar-
velous. They would think of them apart from the trees and apart
from the earth and apart from the sun, which was stupid.

They were mine if I could reach them, but I couldn't. It was
lovely enough only to see them, but I had been looking at them for
weeks. I had seen the trees when they had been bare of leaf. I had
seen the coming of leaves, the coming of blossoms. I had seen blossoms falling away before the pressure of the hard green shapes of
unripe pears.

Now the pears were ripe and ready, and I was ready. I had seen
and the pears were mine, from God.

But it was not to eat. It was to touch and to feel and to know: *the
pear*. Of life—the sum of it—which could decay. It was to know and
to make immortal.

A thief can be both an artist and a philosopher, and probably
should be both. I do not know whether I invented the philosophy
to justify the theft, or whether I denied the existence of theft in
order to invent the philosophy. I know I was deeply sincere about

wanting the ripe pears, and I know I was determined to get them, and to remain innocent.

Afterwards, when they made a thief of me, I weakened and almost believed I *was* a thief, but it was not so.

I laughed, standing beneath those pear boughs, but it was not the laughter of one who destroys and wastes. It was the laughter of one who creates and preserves. An artist is one who looks and sees, and all who have vision are not unblind. I saw the pears. I saw them first with my eyes, and little by little I saw them with every part of my body, and with all of my heart. Therefore, they were mine.

Also, because they existed on branches growing beyond the fence.

A tragic misfortune of youth is that it is speechless when it has the most to say, and a sadness of maturity is that it is garrulous when it has forgotten where to begin and what language to use. Oh, we have been well educated in error, all right. We at least know that we have forgotten.

I couldn't reach them, so I tried leaping, which was and is splendid. At first I leaped with the idea of reaching a branch and lowering it to myself, but after I leaped two or three times I began to leap because it was splendid to leap.

It was like pears being more than pears. It was to get a little way off the earth, upward, inwardly and outwardly, and then to return suddenly to it, with a sound; to be flesh and more than flesh; full of it. And I leaped many times.

I was leaping when I heard the school bell ring, and I remember that at first it sickened me because I knew I was late. A moment afterwards, though, I thought nothing of being late, having as justification both the ripe pears and my discovery of leaping.

I knew it was a reasonable bargain. I forget what they were teaching that day in second grade, but I believe it was hardly more important than my wanting and getting ripe pears, and finding about leaping upward toward pear boughs.

Wholly speechless, though. I didn't stop to think they would ask me, and I would not have the words to say it. I only knew I knew.

I got five pears by using a dead tree twig. There were many more to have, but I chose only five, those that were the most ready. One I ate. Four I took to class, arriving ten minutes late.

A normal man is no less naïve at six than at sixty, but few men are normal. Many are seemingly civilized. Four pears I took to class, showing them as my reason for lateness. I do not remember what I said, if I said anything, but the ripe pears I showed.

This caused instantaneous misunderstanding, and I knew I was being taken for a thief, which was both embarrassing and annoying. I had nothing to say because I had the pears. They were both the evidence and the justification, and I felt bewildered because the pears to Miss Larkin were only the evidence. I had hoped she would have more sense, being a teacher and one who had lived long.

She was severe and said many things. I understood only that she was angry and inclined toward the opinion that I should be punished. The details are blurred but I remember feeling somewhat a thief, waiting for Mr. Pollard, our principal.

The pears were on his table, now certainly only evidence. They were cheerless and I was frightened.

There was nothing else to do; so I ate a pear. It was sweet, sweeter than the one I had eaten by the tree. The core remained in my hand, lingering there in a foolish way. I could not invent an artful thing to do with the core and began fearfully to think: apple core—who for?—Baltimore. And so on. A core should be for throwing, but there were walls around me and windows.

I ate also the core, having only in my hand a number of seeds. These I pocketed, thinking of growing pear trees of my own.

One pear followed another because I was frightened and disliked feeling a thief. It was an unaesthetic experience because I felt no joy.

Mr. Pollard came at last. His coming was like the coming of doom, and when he coughed I thought the whole world shook. He coughed a couple of times, looked at me severely a number of times, and then said: I hear you have been stealing pears. Where are they?

I imagined he wanted to eat a pear, and consequently felt very much ashamed of myself because I had none to give him, but I suppose he took it the other way around and believed I was ashamed because I was a thief who had been caught.

Then I knew I was being punished, because I could see him taking advantage of my shame.

It was not pleasant, either, to hear him say I had stolen, because I hadn't. I saw the pears before they were pears. I saw the bare tree twigs. I saw the leaves and the blossoms, and I kept seeing the pears until they were ready. I *made* them. The ripe ones belonged to me.

I said: I ate them.

It is a pity I could not tell him I didn't steal the pears because I had created them, but I knew how to say only that which others expected me to say.

You *ate* the pears? he said. It seemed to me that he was angry.

Nevertheless, I said: Yes, sir.

How many pears? he said.

Four, I said.

You *stole* four pears, he said, and then *ate* them?

No, sir, I said. Five. One I ate by the tree.

Everything was tangled up, and I knew I wouldn't be able to get out of it. I couldn't think of a thing to say that was my own, and all I could do was answer his questions in a way that would justify his punishing me, which he did.

He gave me a sound licking with a leather strap, and I cried for all I was worth. It didn't hurt so much as my crying made out that it hurt, but I *had* to cry because it seemed very strange to me that no one could even faintly understand why I picked the five pears and carried four of them to class when I could have eaten them instead and made up a lie about helping a stranger find a street or something like that.

I know Miss Larkin is dead, but if old man Pollard is still alive I hope he reads this because I am writing it for him, saying that I did *not* steal the pears, I created them, and took four to class because they were beautiful and I wanted others to see them as I saw them. No hard feelings, Mr. Pollard, but I thought I ought to tell you how it really was with me that day.

The Great Unwritten American Novel

There are two regions. One is on the surface and the other is elsewhere, perhaps everywhere. The first is geographical, Iowa, Manhattan, Ireland, India, Russia, and the house in which you live. This region is the region of things, things seen and things that are and things that are material. It is the region of nations and peoples, patriotism and other forms of vanity.

The second region is not geographical and it is without maps and without kings queens premiers dictators presidents armies and community singing. It is American and it is not American and it is Russian and it is not Russian.

It is breathing.

It is the region of things and the region of things not seen. It is the noblest of all regions and it has always been ignored. It began before the geographical region and it has always been with us and it has always been ignored.

It is seeing. It is being. It is knowing.

Now is the time to cease ignoring it. Now is the time for all good men to cease being unalive and to begin being. Remembrance is of the past in those who live death. It is of the future in those who live being.

There is laughter. I mention this for what it is worth. Recent inhabitants of the earth do not laugh, they weep. Laughter is another thing.

This is not a novel and it is not a poem and it is not a thing for clerks to read while riding the subway to town. This is a conversation.

It is a thing for those who live everywhere.

I will explain this.

West of somewhere is America and east of somewhere is America and north and south. It is the same with all places. America is everywhere and all things are everywhere. There is no sense in saying where a thing is when it is everywhere and it is not wise to say that a man is alive in Chicago and it is not wise because all who are alive are alive in themselves, wherever they go, and it is the customary thing.

There are boundaries. The first boundary is mortality. It is likewise the last boundary and the only boundary. You have a body and limbs. You have fingers and toes and a head. You have a heart and other things. These are the boundaries. Geography begins at home. A man's nose is not a peninsula but it is a projection in space. A man's spirit is not the Atlantic Ocean but it is as wide and as wild.

I mention the simple facts.

II

I mention Ezra Pound.

Is Ezra Pound American? Or is Ezra Pound Ezra Pound?

As I see it Ezra Pound is walking. And he is talking. He is saying in every known language, I am speaking for the man. I am not speaking for men and I am not speaking for mobs. I am ashamed of history and I am amused with the things mobs have done.

Ezra expectorates.

He says, I am saying there is no direction but the direction I am taking and I am taking it alone. There is a chance that when the shouting is over it shall be known that I walked and that I said these things.

As I see it Ezra Pound is walking in the second region.

You may be dead and not aware of it.

III

I mention the editor of the *Saturday Evening Post.* (This is a serious conversation.) I do not know his name and I do not know where he came from and I do not know what he is trying to do or where he is going.

As I see it he is a man called Jones which is the equivalent of X in mathematics.

He has an office and eleven private secretaries and a regiment of clerks. He has a telephone and two hundred filing cabinets and a good suit of clothes.

As I see it he is riding to his desk from a large house in the country. He is a country gentleman. He is a small man and he is riding.

There are three things on his mind. These three things are always on his mind.

He is thinking about America.

He is thinking about the people in America.

He is thinking about five cents.

You do not have to be alive to think about these things.

If Mr. Jones can get one million more Americans to pay five cents for the *Saturday Evening Post* every week he will be very happy because he will be able to charge advertisers more money.

Mr. Jones is an important man.

If there is a war somewhere he can send someone to the scene of the war and have him write an article on it for the *Saturday Evening Post.*

If something happens he can speak of it.

He cannot speak of something before it happens and he cannot speak so that one thing and not another will happen.

Ezra Pound can.

For this reason Mr. Jones is an important man and a patriot.

He thinks of five cents.

Ezra Pound is not important and he is not a patriot because he will not and cannot think of five cents.

IV

Here we have what is called a *situation.*

Ezra Pound, walking in the second region, chances upon Mr. Jones, riding in the first region. (I mention that there is only one true novel. It has never been written because writers have always been in the first region. I am speaking of the novel that must eventually be written. It will have to be about Ezra Pound and the editor of the *Saturday Evening Post.* It will have to be about everything.)

Ezra Pound and Mr. Jones have a brief conversation.

Ezra Pound says, It is likely that you are not ashamed of yourself because you have a large income.

Mr. Jones replies, On the contrary, I am thinking of art. Advertising is an art. Read H. G. Wells.

This is not a moving picture but this scene is one that moves. Mr. Jones is riding. Ezra Pound is walking. It is a bad moving picture because there is no love in it. Mr. Jones does not love Ezra Pound and Ezra Pound does not love Mr. Jones.

There is no leading lady.

The scene fades. Mr. Jones goes on riding and Ezra Pound goes on walking. Historians will mention this in the Twenty-first Century.

It is not the end of the story.

The story begins when Ezra Pound sits down to write a letter to a young poet in Kansas.

This happens just at the moment that Mr. Jones stands up to yawn. It is history.

In the meantime, fifteen million Americans are unemployed.

Have you ever been hungry? Have you ever walked through city streets all night? Have you ever been cold?

V

Every four years a Vice-President is born.

Part of our heritage is art.

Young people should learn to play the violin. There is no substitute for piety. The streets swarm with faces. It is raining everywhere. Everyone lives. There is music on the radio.

VI

Here is a novel. There will be several. It is a writer's novel. It is not the real novel. Anyone who wishes to do so may write this novel, placing the commas in their proper places. This novel is not protected by copyright.

A young man is born in Kansas City. (A young man is born.) He goes to grammar school and learns that it is noble to be honest and he is taught that all great men have been honest. He grows and he goes to high school and is taught that in America every man is free to go as far as he is able. He is taught that it is possible for every man to be a millionaire. He grows and he goes to college and is taught to believe in man. He is taught to read English poetry. Just at the moment when he is ready to begin living among men war is declared and he is placed in a soldier's uniform. (I do not mention his mother because this is a line drawing of one life.) He is not a soldier but he puts on a uniform and crosses the Atlantic. He doesn't like it but he doesn't know what he can do about it. General Pershing is somewhere in the first region and the young man is somewhere in the second region. The young man gets to be twenty-three and then he gets to be killed.

It is a bad novel because there is no love in it.

(I am not mentioning names. I am speaking of the things names represent. When I mention General Pershing I am not speaking of a man at the head of the American Army. I am speaking of our times. I do not wish to suggest that General Pershing is not a great man. It is because I do not believe in him at all. It is because I believe in the young man.)

This novel happened to many young men many times. It happened to Americans, to Germans, to Austrians, Russians, Frenchmen, Englishmen, Poles, Serbs, Italians, Greeks, but it happened mostly to man. Every army has a general. No one has mentioned this novel in the proper way.

I mention it because it ought to be mentioned in a work of this sort.

General Pershing did not get to be killed. He wrote his memoirs and got to be a writer. He got one of the Pulitzer Prizes.

What did he remember? What did he forget? Why is it that generals do not write what they forget?

There is so little love in this novel that it will not please good Americans.

VII

I mention weeds.

O valiant seed of life, there are no dead.

The young men are walking everywhere.

VIII

This is about machinery. The wheel and the piston and the iron finger, the million iron fingers, the million iron minds, the heartless bloodless living steel and the mirage of twirling tons.

Toys are still being made. There are still children. We surely mean something by this. We surely intend some hope. It cannot be blamed on the moving pictures. It is not being blamed on Our Father in Heaven. There is birth. We mean something by this. It is not a question of letters. Everyone stops reading eventually.

Do we fear machinery? Is it possible that we fear steel that turns? Why do we speak so often of junk?

We are worried.

I mention again the children. I refer to their toys: toy automobiles, toy steam-shovels, toy airplanes, toy trucks, toy dirigibles, toy ideas. We manufacture impressions. We produce memories. We present war to savages.

All the machines are running and a lot of men are running. There is confusion. In the cities there have been riots. Is this love?

Hardly any men are walking. Ezra Pound is walking.

There is some starvation. We do not speak of this on feast days. When we have dined we do not speak of starvation. There is some cold.

I mention Rockefeller Center. What do we mean by Rockefeller Center?

In the Great Hall of the RCA Building in Rockefeller Center there will be nine panels; three each by Jose Maria Sert, distinguished Spanish artist, Diego Rivera, distinguished Mexican artist, and Frank Brangwyn, distinguished British artist.

This is history.

Señor Sert arrived in New York on April 22, 1933. He brought with him four sweeping murals. They depict man's mastery of the problem of civilization. They represent the stamping out of forces which destroy life—war, bondage, and disease. (I am quoting from the newspapers.)

Señor Rivera is painting a forthright statement of the Communist viewpoint, unmistakable as such, and intended to be unmistakable, and it is being paid for by John D. Rockefeller, Jr., whose opposition to collectivist principles has been unwavering over a lifetime.

I continue from the newspapers.

Señor Rivera is accustomed to producing sensations with his works. Only recently a bitter controversy was fought over murals he did for the Detroit Institute of Arts. The depiction of the vaccination of a child by his parents was interpreted by some as a caricature of the Holy Family. Nevertheless, the Institute accepted the murals with thanks and congratulated Edsel Ford, the son of Henry, for having the generosity to pay the bill.

The son of Henry. The generosity to pay the bill.

I am a worker, Señor Rivera said to a reporter who climbed his scaffold and sat beside him as he worked.

Equally provocative to a public accustomed to innocuous decoration is a prominent segment, done in the most vivid of earthy reds and browns and greens, showing the greatly magnified germs of diseases. Starting at the top are the microbes given life by poisonous gases used in the War, including anthrax and tuberculosis, and proceeding toward the end are the germs of the infectious and hereditary social diseases, the latter so placed in the composition as to indicate them as the results of a civilization revolving about night clubs and bridge parties.

This is news. It will be good news a hundred years from now.

In the Great Hall of the largest building in gross space in the world is Señor Rivera sitting on the scaffold painting.

Up the scaffold comes Mr. Jones.

You are a Communist, Señor Rivera, he says, but do not forget that except for the multi-millionaires you would never be paid to paint these fearful things.

Señor Rivera is in overalls. Mr. Jones is in his Sunday clothes.

Up the scaffold comes Ezra Pound.

The next war, he says, will be fought with brushes and paint and my continent will conquer the false doctrines of all time.

He moves gently against Mr. Jones, who loses his balance and falls on his face. Three readers of the *Saturday Evening Post* buy the *New Masses*.

Mike Gold goes to lunch.

IX

I mention God.

My theme is not a blasphemous theme. I am not mentioning God as a missionary mentions God. I speak of the God of the second region. The other God is a Presbyterian. Or he is a Baptist. Or he is a Catholic. It isn't worth going on. I am interested in the original. Accept no imitations. Look for the signature. It is thus, on every bottle. Bayer and Castoria, Mr. Fletcher and Dr. Pierce, Lydia Pinkham and the Mid-Western females.

We have our songs.

Yes, we have no music. There is some humming, however. South, mostly. North there is talk. South the black fellows shuffle and hum. It is of the spirit and they are illiterate. North there is no humming and the young people are not illiterate. They read the daily newspapers. Why not? This is a free country, and you foreigners can go back where you came from. Or else. You can go back. Jump in the lake.

You millionaires can jump in the street. These tendencies are inherited. A heavy man can fall forty stories in less than forty seconds, any day of the week. The airplane is slower and death is not always instantaneous. No parachutes for bankers. The open window and the sidewalk. This is no dream.

A certain amount of grace is inevitable, even among rodents. A good rabbit has its manners.

X

Up the scaffold comes Emiliano Zapata, the peon martyr. He speaks in Mexican to Señor Rivera.

Señor, he says, let us not forget humility. Let us remember God.

Up the scaffold comes Felipe Carrillo, the martyr.

Amigo, he says, we must forgive.

Up the scaffold comes Cuahuatemoc, the martyr.

Brother, he says, we have not yet learned to pray. Let us paint the prayers of our people.

Up the scaffold comes Montano, the martyr. He is a young man who is smiling.

Diego, Diego, he says, God bless you, God bless you. You have not forgotten to pray. You are on your knees always.

Montano and the other martyrs kneel beside Señor Rivera.

There is Mexican praying in the Great Hall at Rockefeller Center. It is not mentioned in the news stories.

Ezra Pound writes another letter to another young poet. Remember, he writes, to be lucid. Don't say what you don't mean and don't mean what you don't say. Speak English. Some people still understand the language.

I mention everything, and this is the Great Unwritten American Novel, or else.

Antranik of Armenia

I didn't learn to speak Armenian until my grandmother came to our house and every morning sang about Antranik the soldier until I knew he was an Armenian, a mountain peasant on a black horse who with only a handful of men was fighting the enemy. That was in 1915, the year of physical pain and spiritual disintegration for the people of my country, and the people of the world, but I was seven and I didn't know. From my own meaningless grief I could imagine something was wrong in the world, but I didn't know what. My grandmother sang in a way that made me begin to find out, singing mournfully and with great anger, in a strong voice, while she worked in the house. I picked up the language in no time because it was in me in the first place and all I needed to do was fit the words to the remembrance. I was an Armenian. God damn the bastards who were making the trouble. (That is the way it is when you are an Armenian, and it is wrong. There are no bastards. The bitter feeling of the Armenian is also the bitter feeling of the Turk. It is all absurd, but I did not know. I did not know the Turk is a simple, amiable, helpless man who does what he is forced to do. I did not know that hating him was the same as hating the Armenian since they were the same. My grandmother didn't know either, and still does not know. I know now, but I don't know what good it is going to do me because there is still idiocy in the world and by idiocy I mean everything lousy, like ignorance and, what is still worse, willful blindness. Everybody in the world knows there is no such thing as nationality, but look at them. Look at Germany, Italy, France, England. Look at Russia even. Look at Poland. Just look at all the crazy maniacs. I can't figure out why they won't open their eyes and see that it is all idiocy. I can't figure out why they won't learn to use

their strength for life instead of death, but it looks as if they won't.
My grandmother is too old to learn, but how about all the people
in the world who were born less than thirty years ago? How about
all those people? Are they too young to learn? Or is it proper to
work only for death?)

In 1915 General Antranik was part of the cause of the trouble in
the world, but it wasn't his fault. There was no other way out for
him and he was doing only what he had to do. The Turks were
killing Armenians and General Antranik and his soldiers were
killing Turks. He was killing fine, simple, amiable Turks, but he
wasn't destroying any real criminal because every real criminal was
far from the scene of fighting. An eye for an eye, but always the
wrong eye. And my grandmother prayed for the triumph and safety
of General Antranik, although she knew Turks were good people.
She herself said they were.

General Antranik had the same job in Armenia and Turkey that
Lawrence of Arabia had in Arabia: to harass the Turkish Army and
keep it from being a menace to the armies of Italy and France and
England. General Antranik was a simple Armenian peasant who
believed the governments of England and France and Italy when
these governments told him his people would be given their freedom for making trouble for the Turkish Army. He was not an
adventurous and restless English writer who was trying to come to
terms with himself as to what was valid in the world for him, and
unlike Lawrence of Arabia General Antranik did not know that
what he was doing was stupid and futile because after the trouble
the governments of England and France and Italy would betray
him. He did not know a strong government needs and seeks the
friendship of another strong government, and after the war there
was nothing in the world for him or the people of Armenia. The
strong governments talked about doing something for Armenia,
but they never did anything. And the war was over and General
Antranik was only a soldier, not a soldier and a diplomat and a
writer. He was only an Armenian. He didn't fight the Turkish Army
because it would give him something to write about. He didn't write
two words about the whole war. He fought the Turkish Army because
he was an Armenian. When the war ended and the fine diplomatic

negotiating began General Antranik was lost, the Turkish government looked upon him as a criminal and offered a large sum of
money for his capture, dead or alive. General Antranik escaped to
Bulgaria, but Turkish patriots followed him to Bulgaria, so he came
to America.

General Antranik came to my home town. It looked as if all the
Armenians in California were at the Southern Pacific depot the day
he arrived. I climbed a telephone pole and saw him when he got off
the train. He was a man of about fifty in a neat American suit of
clothes. He was a little under six feet tall, very solid and very strong.
He had an old-style Armenian moustache that was white. The
expression of his face was both ferocious and kindly. The people
swallowed him up and a committee got him into a great big
Cadillac and drove away with him.

I got down from the telephone pole and ran all the way to my
uncle's office. That was in 1919 or 1920, and I was eleven or twelve.
Maybe it was a year or two later. It doesn't make any difference.
Anyway, I was working in my uncle's office as office boy. All I used
to do was go out and get him a cold watermelon once in a while
which he used to cut in the office, right on his desk. He used to eat
the big half and I used to eat the little half. If a client came to see
him while he was eating watermelon, I would tell the client my
uncle was very busy and ask him to wait in the reception room or
come back in an hour. Those were the days for me and my uncle. He
was a lawyer with a good practice and I was his nephew, his sister's
son, as well as a reader of books. We used to talk in Armenian and
English and spit the seeds into the cuspidor.

My uncle was sitting at his desk, all excited, smoking a cigarette.

Did you see Antranik? he said in Armenian.

In Armenian we never called him General Antranik, only in
English.

I saw him, I said.

My uncle was very excited. Here, he said. Here's a quarter. Go and
get a big cold watermelon.

When I came back with the watermelon there were four men
in the office, the editor of the *Asbarez,* another lawyer, and two
clients, farmers. They were all smoking cigarettes and talking about

Antranik. My uncle gave me a dollar and told me to go and get as many more watermelons as I could carry. I came back with a big watermelon under each arm and my uncle cut each melon in half and each of us had half a melon to eat. There were only two big spoons and one butter knife, so the two farmers ate with their fingers, and so did I.

My uncle represented one of the farmers, and the other lawyer represented the other. My uncle's client said he had loaned two hundred dollars to the other farmer three years ago but had neglected to get a note, and the other farmer said he had never borrowed a penny from anybody. That was the argument, but nobody was bothering about it now. We were all eating watermelon and being happy about Antranik. At last the other attorney said, About this little matter?

My uncle squirted some watermelon seeds from his mouth into the cuspidor and turned to the other lawyer's client.

Did Hovsep lend you two hundred dollars three years ago? he said.

Yes, that is true, said the other farmer.

He dug out a big chunk of the heart of the watermelon with his fingers and pushed it into his mouth.

But yesterday, said the other lawyer, you told me he didn't lend you a penny.

That was yesterday, said the farmer. Today I saw Antranik. I have no money now, but I will pay him just as soon as I sell my crop.

Brother, said the farmer named Hovsep to the other farmer, that's all I wanted to know. I loaned you two hundred dollars because you needed the money, and I wanted you to pay me so people wouldn't laugh at me for being a fool. Now it is different. I don't want you to pay me. It is a gift to you. I don't need the money.

No, brother, said the other farmer, a debt is a debt. I insist upon paying.

My uncle swallowed watermelon, listening to the two farmers.

I don't want the money, said the farmer named Hovsep.

I borrowed two hundred dollars from you, didn't I? said the other farmer.

Yes.

Then I must pay you back.

No, brother, I will not accept the money.

But you must.

No.

The other farmer turned to his lawyer bitterly. Can we take the case to court and make him take the money? he said.

The other lawyer looked at my uncle whose mouth was full of watermelon. He looked at my uncle in a way that was altogether comical and Armenian, meaning, Well, what the hell do you call this? and my uncle almost choked with laughter and watermelon and seeds.

Then all of us busted out laughing, even the two farmers.

Countrymen, said my uncle. Go home. Forget this unimportant matter. This is a great day for us. Our hero Antranik has come to us from Hairenik, our native land. Go home and be happy.

The two farmers went away, talking together about the great event.

Every Armenian in California was happy about the arrival of Antranik from the old country.

One day six or seven months later Antranik came to my uncle's office when I was there. I knew he had visited my uncle many times while I was away from the office, in school, but this was the first time I had seen him so closely, he himself, the man, our great national hero General Antranik, in the very room where I sat with my uncle. I felt very angry and sad because I could see how bewildered and bitter and disappointed he was. Where was the glorious new Armenia he had dreamed of winning for his people? Where was the magnificent resurrection of the ancient race?

He came into the office quietly, almost shyly, as only a great man can be quiet and shy, and my uncle jumped up from his desk, loving him more than he loved any other man in the world, and through him loving the lost nation, the multitude dead, and the multitude living in every alien corner of the world. And I with my uncle, jumping up and loving him the same way, but him only, Antranik, the great man fallen to nothing, the soldier helpless in a world now full of cheap and false peace, he himself betrayed and his people betrayed, and Armenia only a memory.

He talked quietly for about an hour and then went away, and when I looked at my uncle I saw that tears were in his eyes and his mouth was twisting with agony like the mouth of a small boy who is in great pain but will not let himself cry.

That was what came of our little part in the bad business of 1915, and it will be the same with other nations, great and small, for many years to come because that way is the bad way, the wasteful way, and even if your nation is strong enough to win the war, death of one sort or another is the only ultimate consequence, death, not life, is the only end, and it is always people, not nations, because it is all one nation, the living, so why won't they change the way? Why do they want to go on fooling themselves? They know there are a lot of finer ways to be strong than to be strong in numbers, in war, so why don't they cut it out? What do they want to do to all the fine, amiable, simple people of every nation in the world? The Turk is the brother of the Armenian and they know it. The German and the Frenchman, the Russian and the Pole, the Japanese and the Chinese. They are all brothers. They are all small tragic entities of mortality. Why do they want them to kill one another? What good does it do anybody?

I like the swell exhilaration that comes from having one's body and mind in opposition to some strong force, but why should that force be one's own brothers instead of something less subject to the agonies of mortality? Why can't the God damn war be a nobler kind of war? Is every noble problem of man solved? Is there nothing more to do but kill? Everybody knows there are other things to do, so why won't they cut out the monkey business?

The governments of strong nations betrayed Antranik and Armenia after the war, but the soldiers of Armenia refused to betray themselves. It was no joke with them. It would be better to be dead, they said, than to be betrayed by their own intelligence into new submission. To fight was to be impractical, but not to fight was to be racially nullified. They knew it would be suicide because they had no friend in the world. The governments of strong nations were busy with complex diplomatic problems of their own. Their war was ended and the time had come for conversation. For the soldiers of Armenia the time had come for death or great good fortune, and the Armenian is too wise to believe in great good fortune.

These were the Nationalists, the *Tashnaks,* and they fought for
Armenia, for the nation Armenia, because it was the only way they
knew how to fight for life and dignity and race. The world had no
other way. It was with guns only. The diplomats had no time for
Armenia. It was the bad way, the God damn lousy way, but these
men were great men and they did what they had to do, and any
Armenian who despises these men is either ignorant or a traitor to
his race. These men were dead wrong. I know they were dead
wrong, but it was the only way. Well, they won the war. (No war is
ever won: that is a technical term, used solely to save space and
time.) Somehow or other the whole race was not annihilated. The
people of Armenia were cold and hungry and ill, but these soldiers
won their war and Armenia was a nation with a government, a
political party, the *Tashnaks.* (That is so sad, that is so pathetic when
you think of the thousands who were killed, but I honor the soldiers, those who died and those who still live. These I honor and
love, and all who compromised I only love.) It was a ghastly mistake, but it was a noble mistake, and Armenia was Armenia. It was
a very small nation of course, a very unimportant nation, surrounded on all sides by enemies, but for two years Armenia was
Armenia, and the capital was Erivan. For the first time in thousands
of years Armenia was Armenia.

I know how silly it is to be proud, but I cannot help it, I am
proud.

The war was with the Turks of course. The other enemies were
less active than the Turks, but watchful. When the time came one
of these, in the name of love, not hate, accomplished in no time at
all what the Turks, who were more honest, whose hatred was
unconcealed, could not accomplish in hundreds of years. These
were the Russians. The new ones. They were actually the old ones,
but they had a new theory and they said their idea was brotherhood on earth. They made a brother of Armenia at the point of a
gun, but even so, if brotherhood was really their idea, that's all
right. They killed all the leaders of the Armenian soldiers, but
nobody will hold that against them either. Very few of the
Armenians of Armenia wanted to be brothers to the new Russians,

but each of them was hungry and weary of the war and consequently the revolt against the new enemy was brief and tragic. It
ended in no time at all. It looked like the world simply wouldn't let
the Armenians have their own country, even after thousands of
years, even after more than half of the Armenians of Asia Minor
had been killed. They just didn't want the Armenians to have their
nation. So it turned out that the leaders of the Armenian soldiers
were criminals, so they were shot. That's all. The Russian brothers
just shot them. Then they told the Armenians not to be afraid, the
Turks wouldn't bother them any more. The brotherly Russian soldiers marched through the streets of the cities of Armenia and told
everybody not to be afraid. Every soldier had a gun. There was a
feeling of great brotherliness in Armenia.

Away out in California I sat in my uncle's office. To hell with it,
I said. It's all over. We can begin to forget Armenia now. Antranik is
dead. The nation is lost. The strong nations of the world are jumping with new problems. To hell with the whole God damn mess,
I said. I'm no Armenian. I'm an American.

Well, the truth is I am both and neither. I love Armenia and I
love America and I belong to both, but I am only this: an inhabitant
of the earth, and so are you, whoever you are.

I tried to forget Armenia but I couldn't do it. My birthplace was
California, but I couldn't forget Armenia, so what is one's country?
Is it land of the earth, in a specific place? Rivers there? Lakes? The
sky there? The way the moon comes up there? And the sun? Is
one's country the trees, the vineyards, the grass, the birds, the rocks,
the hills and mountains and valleys? Is it the temperature of the
place in spring and summer and winter? Is it the animal rhythm of
the living there? The huts and houses, the streets of cities, the tables
and chairs, and the drinking of tea and talking? Is it the peach
ripening in summer heat on the bough? Is it the dead in the earth
there? The unborn of love beginning? Is it the sound of the spoken
language in all the places of that country under the sky? The printed
word of that language? The picture painted there? The song of that
throat and heart? That dance? Is one's country their prayers of
thanks for air and water and earth and fire and life? Is it their eyes?
Their lips smiling? The grief?

Well, I do not know for sure, but I know it is all these things as remembrance in the blood. It is all these things within one's self, because I have been there, I have been to Armenia and I have seen with my own eyes, and I know. I have been to the place. Armenia. There is no nation there, but that is all the better. But I have been to that place, and I know this: that there is no nation in the world, no England and France and Italy, and no nation whatsoever. And I know that each who lives upon the earth is no more than a tragic entity of mortality, let him be king or beggar. I would like to see them awaken to this truth and stop killing one another because I believe there are other and finer ways to be great and brave and exhilarated. I believe there are ways whose ends are life instead of death. What difference does it make what the nation is or what political theory governs it? Does that in any way decrease for its subjects the pain and sorrow of mortality? Or in any way increase the strength and delight?

I went to see. To find out. To breathe that air. To be in that place.

The grapes of the Armenian vineyards were not yet ripe, but there were fresh green leaves, and the vines were exactly like the vines of California, and the faces of the Armenians of Armenia were exactly like the faces of the Armenians of California. The rivers Arax and Kura moved slowly through the fertile earth of Armenia in the same way that the rivers King and San Joaquin moved through the valley of my birthplace. And the sun was warm and kindly, no less than the sun of California.

And it was nowhere and everywhere. It was different and exactly the same, word for word, pebble for pebble, leaf for leaf, eye for eye and tooth for tooth. It was neither Armenia nor Russia. It was people alive in that place, and not people only, but all things alive there, animate and inanimate: the vines, the trees, the rocks, the rivers, the streets, the buildings, the whole place, urban and rural, nowhere and everywhere. The earth again. And it was sad. The automobile bounced over the dirt road to the ancient Armenian church at Aitchmiadzin, and the peasants, men and women and children, stood in bare feet on the ancient stone floor, looking up at the cross, bowing their heads, and believing. And the Armenian students of Marx laughed humbly and a little shamefully at the innocent unwisdom and foolish faith of their brothers. And the sadness of Armenia, my country, was so great in me that, sitting in the automobile, returning to Erivan, the only thing I could remember about Armenia was the quiet way General Antranik talked with my uncle many years ago and the tears in my uncle's eyes when he was gone, and the painful way my uncle's lips were twisting.

The Summer of the Beautiful White Horse

One day back there in the good old days when I was nine and the world was full of every imaginable kind of magnificence, and life was still a delightful and mysterious dream, my cousin Mourad, who was considered crazy by everybody who knew him except me, came to my house at four in the morning and woke me up by tapping on the window of my room.

Aram, he said.

I jumped out of bed and looked out the window.

I couldn't believe what I saw.

It wasn't morning yet, but it was summer and with daybreak not many minutes around the corner of the world it was light enough for me to know I wasn't dreaming.

My cousin Mourad was sitting on a beautiful white horse.

I stuck my head out of the window and rubbed my eyes.

Yes, he said in Armenian. It's a horse. You're not dreaming. Make it quick if you want to ride.

I knew my cousin Mourad enjoyed being alive more than anybody else who had ever fallen into the world by mistake, but this was more than even I could believe.

In the first place, my earliest memories had been memories of horses and my first longings had been longings to ride.

This was the wonderful part.

In the second place, we were poor.

This was the part that wouldn't permit me to believe what I saw.

We were poor. We had no money. Our whole tribe was poverty-stricken. Every branch of the Garoghlanian family was living in the most amazing and comical poverty in the world. Nobody could understand where we ever got money enough to keep us with food in our bellies, not even the old men of the family. Most important of all, though, we were famous for our honesty. We had been famous for our honesty for something like eleven centuries, even when we had been the wealthiest family in what we liked to think was the world. We were proud first, honest next, and after that we believed in right and wrong. None of us would take advantage of anybody in the world, let alone steal.

Consequently, even though I could *see* the horse, so magnificent; even though I could *smell* it, so lovely; even though I could *hear* it breathing, so exciting; I couldn't *believe* the horse had anything to do with my cousin Mourad or with me or with any of the other members of our family, asleep or awake, because I *knew* my cousin Mourad couldn't have *bought* the horse, and if he couldn't have bought it he must have *stolen* it, and I refused to believe he had stolen it.

No member of the Garoghlanian family could be a thief.

I stared, first at my cousin and then at the horse. There was a pious stillness and humor in each of them which on the one hand delighted me and on the other frightened me.

Mourad, I said, where did you steal this horse?

Leap out of the window, he said, if you want to ride.

It was true, then. He *had* stolen the horse. There was no question about it. He had come to invite me to ride or not, as I chose.

Well, it seemed to me stealing a horse for a ride was not the same thing as stealing something else, such as money. For all I knew, maybe it wasn't stealing at all. If you were crazy about horses the way my cousin Mourad and I were, it wasn't stealing. It wouldn't become stealing until we offered to sell the horse, which of course I knew we would never do.

Let me put on some clothes, I said.

All right, he said, but hurry.

I leaped into my clothes.

I jumped down to the yard from the window and leaped up onto the horse behind my cousin Mourad.

That year we lived at the edge of town, on Walnut Avenue. Behind our house was the country: vineyards, orchards, irrigation ditches, and country roads. In less than three minutes we were on Olive Avenue, and then the horse began to trot. The air was new and lovely to breathe. The feel of the horse running was wonderful. My cousin Mourad who was considered one of the craziest members of our family began to sing. I mean, he began to roar.

Every family has a crazy streak in it somewhere, and my cousin Mourad was considered the natural descendant of the crazy streak in our tribe. Before him was our uncle Khosrove, an enormous man with a powerful head of black hair and the largest mustache in the San Joaquin Valley, a man so furious in temper, so irritable, so impatient that he stopped anyone from talking by roaring, *It is no harm; pay no attention to it.*

That was all, no matter what anybody happened to be talking about. Once it was his own son Arak running eight blocks to the barber shop where his father was having his mustache trimmed to tell him their house was on fire. This man Khosrove sat up in the chair and roared, It is no harm; pay no attention to it. The barber said, But the boy says your house is on fire. So Khosrove roared, Enough, it is no harm, I say.

My cousin Mourad was considered the natural descendant of this man, although Mourad's father was Zorab, who was practical and nothing else. That's how it was in our tribe. A man could be the father of his son's flesh, but that did not mean that he was also the father of his spirit. The distribution of the various kinds of spirit of our tribe had been from the beginning capricious and vagrant.

We rode and my cousin Mourad sang. For all anybody knew we were still in the old country where, at least according to some of our neighbors, we belonged. We let the horse run as long as it felt like running.

At last my cousin Mourad said, Get down. I want to ride alone.

Will you let me ride alone? I said.

That is up to the horse, my cousin said. Get down.

The *horse* will let me ride, I said.

We shall see, he said. Don't forget that I have a way with a horse.

Well, I said, any way you have with a horse, I have also.

For the sake of your safety, he said, let us hope so. Get down.

All right, I said, but remember you've got to let me try to ride alone.

I got down and my cousin Mourad kicked his heels into the horse and shouted, *Vazire*, run. The horse stood on its hind legs, snorted, and burst into a fury of speed that was the loveliest thing I had ever seen. My cousin Mourad raced the horse across a field of dry grass to an irrigation ditch, crossed the ditch on the horse, and five minutes later returned, dripping wet.

The sun was coming up.

Now it's my turn to ride, I said.

My cousin Mourad got off the horse.

Ride, he said.

I leaped to the back of the horse and for a moment knew the awfulest fear imaginable. The horse did not move.

Kick into his muscles, my cousin Mourad said. What are you waiting for? We've got to take him back before everybody in the world is up and about.

I kicked into the muscles of the horse. Once again it reared and snorted. Then it began to run. I didn't know what to do. Instead of running across the field to the irrigation ditch the horse ran down the road to the vineyard of Dikran Halabian where it began to leap over vines. The horse leaped over seven vines before I fell. Then it continued running.

My cousin Mourad came running down the road.

I'm not worried about you, he shouted. We've got to get that horse. You go this way and I'll go this way. If you come upon him, be kindly. I'll be near.

I continued down the road and my cousin Mourad went across the field toward the irrigation ditch.

It took him half an hour to find the horse and bring him back.

All right, he said, jump on. The whole world is awake now.

What will we do? I said.

Well, he said, we'll either take him back or hide him until tomorrow morning.

He didn't sound worried and I knew he'd hide him and not take him back. Not for a while, at any rate.

Where will we hide him? I said.

I know a place, he said.

How long ago did you steal this horse? I said.

It suddenly dawned on me that he had been taking these early morning rides for some time and had come for me this morning only because he knew how much I longed to ride.

Who said anything about stealing a horse? he said.

Anyhow, I said, how long ago did you begin riding every morning?

Not until this morning, he said.

Are you telling the truth? I said.

Of course not, he said, but if we are found out, that's what you're to say. I don't want both of us to be liars. All you know is that we started riding this morning.

All right, I said.

He walked the horse quietly to the barn of a deserted vineyard which at one time had been the pride of a farmer named Fetvajian. There were some oats and dry alfalfa in the barn.

We began walking home.

It wasn't easy, he said, to get the horse to behave so nicely. At first it wanted to run wild, but, as I've told you, I have a way with a horse. I can get it to want to do anything *I* want it to do. Horses understand me.

How do you do it? I said.

I have an understanding with a horse, he said.

Yes, but what sort of an understanding? I said.

A simple and honest one, he said.

Well, I said, I wish I knew how to reach an understanding like that with a horse.

You're still a small boy, he said. When you get to be thirteen you'll know how to do it.

I went home and ate a hearty breakfast.

That afternoon my uncle Khosrove came to our house for coffee and cigarettes. He sat in the parlor, sipping and smoking and remembering the old country. Then another visitor arrived, a farmer named John Byro, an Assyrian who, out of loneliness, had learned to speak Armenian. My mother brought the lonely visitor coffee and tobacco and he rolled a cigarette and sipped and smoked, and then at last, sighing sadly, he said, My white horse which was stolen last month is still gone. I cannot understand it.

My uncle Khosrove became very irritated and shouted, It's no harm. What is the loss of a horse? Haven't we all lost the homeland? What is this crying over a horse?

That may be all right for you, a city dweller, to say, John Byro said, but what of my surrey? What good is a surrey without a horse?

Pay no attention to it, my uncle Khosrove roared.

I walked ten miles to get here, John Byro said.

You have legs, my uncle Khosrove shouted.

My left leg pains me, the farmer said.

Pay no attention to it, my uncle Khosrove roared.

That horse cost me sixty dollars, the farmer said.

I spit on money, my uncle Khosrove said.

He got up and stalked out of the house, slamming the screen door. My mother explained.

He has a gentle heart, she said. It is simply that he is homesick and such a large man.

The farmer went away and I ran over to my cousin Mourad's house.

He was sitting under a peach tree, trying to repair the hurt wing of a young robin which could not fly. He was talking to the bird.

What is it? he said.

The farmer, John Byro, I said. He visited our house. He wants his horse. You've had it a month. I want you to promise not to take it back until I learn to ride.

It will take you *a year* to learn to ride, my cousin Mourad said.

We could keep the horse a year, I said.

My cousin Mourad leaped to his feet.

What? he roared. Are you inviting a member of the Garoghlanian family to steal? The horse must go back to its true owner.

When? I said.

In six months at the latest, he said.

He threw the bird into the air. The bird tried hard, almost fell twice, but at last flew away, high and straight.

Early every morning for two weeks my cousin Mourad and I took the horse out of the barn of the deserted vineyard where we were hiding it and rode it, and every morning the horse, when it was my turn to ride alone, leaped over grape vines and small trees and threw me and ran away. Nevertheless, I hoped in time to learn to ride the way my cousin Mourad rode.

One morning on the way to Fetvajian's deserted vineyard we ran into the farmer John Byro who was on his way to town.

Let me do the talking, my cousin Mourad said. I have a way with farmers.

Good morning, John Byro, my cousin Mourad said to the farmer.

The farmer studied the horse eagerly.

Good morning, sons of my friends, he said. What is the name of your horse?

My Heart, my cousin Mourad said in Armenian.

A lovely name, John Byro said, for a lovely horse. I could swear it is the horse that was stolen from me many weeks ago. May I look into its mouth?

The farmer looked into the mouth of the horse.

Tooth for tooth, he said. I would swear it is my horse if I didn't know your parents. The fame of your family for honesty is well known to me. Yet the horse is the twin of my horse. A suspicious man would believe his eyes instead of his heart. Good day, my young friends.

Good day, John Byro, my cousin Mourad said.

Early the following morning we took the horse to John Byro's vineyard and put it in the barn. The dogs followed us around without making a sound.

The dogs, I whispered to my cousin Mourad. I thought they would bark.

They would at somebody else, he said. I have a way with dogs.

My cousin Mourad put his arms around the horse, pressed his nose into the horse's nose, patted it, and then we went away.

That afternoon John Byro came to our house in his surrey and showed my mother the horse that had been stolen and returned.

I do not know what to think, he said. The horse is stronger than ever. Better-tempered, too. I thank God.

My uncle Khosrove, who was in the parlor, became irritated and shouted, Quiet, man, quiet. Your horse has been returned. Pay no attention to it.

Tracy's Tiger

CHAPTER 1

Thomas Tracy had a tiger.

It was actually a black panther, but that's no matter, because he *thought* of it as a tiger.

It had white teeth.

This is how he came to get his tiger:

When he was three and went by the sound of things somebody said *tiger!* Whatever a *tiger!* was, Tracy wanted his own.

One day he was walking in town with his father when he saw something in the window of a fish restaurant.

"Buy me that tiger," he said.

"That's a lobster," his father said.

"I don't want it, then," Tracy said.

Several years later Tracy visited the zoo with his mother and saw a real tiger in a cage. It was something like the tiger of the word, but it wasn't *his* tiger.

For years Tracy saw pictures of all kinds of animals in dictionaries, paintings, encyclopaedias, and movies. Among these animals stalked many black panthers, but not once did Tracy think of one of them as his own tiger.

One day, however, Tracy was at the zoo alone, fifteen years of age, smoking a cigarette and leering at girls, when all of a sudden he came face to face with *his* tiger.

It was a sleeping black panther that instantly awoke, raised its head, stared straight at Tracy, got to its feet, hummed the way black panthers do, saying something that sounded like *Eyeej*, walked to the edge of the cage, stood for a moment looking at Tracy, then wandered back to the platform on which it had been sleeping. There it plopped down again and began to stare far out into space, as many miles and years out into space as there are miles and years in space.

Tracy in turn stood staring at the black panther. He stared five minutes, chucked away his cigarette, cleared his throat, spat, and walked out of the zoo.

"That's my tiger," he said.

He never went back to the zoo to have another look at his tiger because he didn't need to. He'd got it. He'd got it whole in the five minutes he'd watched it staring into infinity with a tiger's terrible resignation and pride.

CHAPTER 2

When he was twenty-one Tracy and his tiger went to New York, where Tracy took a job at Otto Seyfang's, a coffee importer's on Warren Street in Washington Market. Most of the other businesses of that area were produce houses, so that besides having free coffee to drink—in the Tasting Department—Tracy had free fruit and vegetables to eat.

The pay for the unskilled work Tracy did was poor, but the work was good and hard. It was not easy at first for Tracy to throw a sack of coffee beans weighing a hundred pounds over his shoulder and walk fifty yards with it, but after a week it was nothing at all, and even the tiger marveled at the ease with which Tracy threw the stuff around.

One day Tracy went to his immediate superior, a man named Valora, to discuss his future.

"I want to be a taster," Tracy said.

"Who ast you?" Valora said.

"Who ast me *what?*"

"Who ast you to be a taster?"

"Nobody."

"What do you know about tasting?" Valora said.

"I *like* coffee," Tracy said.

"What do you know about tasting?" Valora said again.

"I've done a little in the Tasting Department."

"You had coffee and doughnuts in the Tasting Department, the same as all the others who ain't professional tasters," Valora said.

"When the coffee was good I knew it," Tracy said. "When it was bad I knew it."

"How did you know?"

"By tasting."

"We got three tasters—Nimmo, Peberdy, and Ringert," Valora said. "They been with Otto Seyfang's twenty-five, thirty-five, forty-one years. How long you been with the firm?"

"Two weeks."

"You want to be a taster?"

"Yes, sir."

"You want to get to the top of the ladder in two weeks?"

"Yes, sir."

"You don't want to wait your turn?"

"No, sir."

At this moment Otto Seyfang himself came into Valora's office. Valora jumped up from his chair, but Otto Seyfang, a man of seventy, wouldn't have it—the jumping up, that is—and he said, "Sit down, Valora! Go ahead!"

"Go ahead?" Valora said.

"Now, go ahead where I interrupted and don't act dumb," Otto Seyfang said.

"We was talking about this new man applying for a job as taster."

"Go ahead."

"He's been here two weeks, and he wants to be a taster."

"Go ahead and talk about it," Otto Seyfang said.

"Yes, sir," Valora said. He turned to Tracy. "After only two weeks," he said, "you want a job that Nimmo, Peberdy, and Ringert didn't get until they was with the firm twenty, twenty-five, thirty years? Is that right?"

"Yes, sir," Tracy said.

"You want to come in here to Otto Seyfang's just like that and get the best job?"

"Yes, sir."

"You know all about coffee tasting?"

"Yes, sir."

"What's good coffee taste like?"

"Coffee."

"What's the *best* coffee taste like?"

"Good coffee."

"What's the difference between *good* coffee and the *best* coffee?"

"Advertising," Tracy said.

Valora turned to Otto Seyfang as much as to say, "What are you going to do with a wise guy like this from out of town?" But Otto Seyfang didn't encourage Valora's attitude. He just waited for Valora to go on.

"They ain't no opening in the Tasting Department," Valora said.

"When *will* there be an opening?" Tracy said.

"Just as soon as Nimmo dies," Valora said. "But there are thirty-nine others at Otto Seyfang's who are ahead of you for the job."

"Nimmo won't die for some time," Tracy said.

"I'll tell him to hurry," Valora said.

"I don't want Nimmo to hurry."

"But you want his job?"

"No, sir," Tracy said. "I want *four* tasters in the Tasting Department."

"*You* want to be the fourth?" Valora said. "Not Shively, who's next in line?"

"What line?"

"The coffee tasters' line," Valora said. "You want to step in ahead of Shively?"

"I don't want to step in ahead of him," Tracy said. "I want to step over to the side into the Tasting Department, because I *can* taste coffee, and I know when it's good."

"You do?"

"Yes, sir."

"Where you from?" Valora said.

"San Francisco," Tracy said.

"Why don't you go back to San Francisco?"

Valora turned to Otto Seyfang.

"That's about it, isn't it, sir?" he said.

Valora didn't know, and neither did Otto Seyfang, that it was Tracy's tiger that had done the talking. They thought it had been Tracy himself.

At first Otto Seyfang believed he might do something surprising that he had seen happen in a stage play once. Surprising, that is, to Valora, and perhaps even to Tracy. But after a while he decided he wasn't in any stage play, he was in his coffee importing house and open for business, not art. He had believed he would hire a fourth coffee taster at that, Tracy himself, because Tracy had had guts enough to go up to Valora and tell him the truth: that he, Tracy, knew good coffee when he, Tracy, tasted it, and on top of that to make known that he, Tracy, had ideas in his head. Advertising, for instance. (What a joke art is when you get right down to it, Otto Seyfang thought. Just because a boy from California comes back with quick answers to an imbecile's questions, in art you're supposed to give the boy what he asks for, and make something of him. But what was the boy *actually*? Was he a coffee man? Did he live and breathe coffee? No. He was a smart aleck.)

Thus, Otto Seyfang decided against doing anything surprising.

"What's your work?" Otto Seyfang said to Tracy.

"I'm a song writer," Tracy said.

"Ah! What's your work at *Otto Seyfang's*?" the old man said. "Do you know who I am?"

"No, sir," Tracy said. "Who are you?"

"Otto Seyfang."

"Do you know who I am?" Tracy said.

"Who are you?"

"Thomas Tracy."

(*I've got this company,* Otto Seyfang thought. *I've had it forty-five years. What have you got?*)

(*I've got a tiger,* Tracy thought in reply to Otto Seyfang's thought.)

They went on talking, but first these thoughts were neatly exchanged.

"What's your work at Otto Seyfang's?" the old man said.

"I throw and carry the sacks," Tracy said.

"Do you want to keep your job?" Otto Seyfang said.

Tracy knew what the tiger was going to say and he was eagerly waiting for the tiger to say it when he discovered that the tiger had fallen asleep from boredom.

Tracy soon heard himself say, "Yes, sir, I want to keep my job."

"Then get the hell back to your work," Otto Seyfang said. "And if you ever waste Valora's time again by coming in here to talk nonsense, I'll fire you. Valora knows how to waste his own time without any help from you. Don't you, Valora?"

"Yes, sir," Valora said.

Tracy went back to his work, leaving the tiger fast asleep under Valora's desk.

When the tiger woke up and went back to Tracy, Tracy wouldn't speak to it.

"Eyeej," the tiger said in the hope of breaking the ice.

"Eyeej my foot," Tracy said. "That was a nice trick to play on a pal. I thought you were going to kick it around. I didn't think you were going to fall asleep. When he said do you want to keep your job, I thought you were going to say something sensible. You call yourself a tiger?"

"Moyl," the tiger murmured.

"Moyl," Tracy said. "Go away."

Tracy threw the sacks in angry silence the rest of the day, for never before had the tiger fallen asleep at a time so appropriate for bad manners, and Tracy didn't like it. He was deeply troubled about the probability of a dubious strain in the tiger's lineage.

After work that day Tracy walked with Nimmo to the subway. Nimmo was nervous all the way there from having tasted coffee all day. Nimmo was almost as old as Otto Seyfang himself and Nimmo had no tiger, had in fact no idea there *were* tigers to be had. All Nimmo was doing was standing in Shively's way. And Shively was standing in the way of the thirty-eight others at Otto Seyfang's.

Well, Tracy had gone to work, but at the same time he had also written three lines to a song. He would go on working at Otto Seyfang's for a while, waiting for the tiger to snap out of it, but he would stand in nobody's way and in nobody's line.

When Tracy got off the subway and went up to Broadway he decided to have a cup of coffee, and he *had* a cup. He was an expert taster, and knew it. He just didn't want to wait any thirty-five years to prove it. He drank a second cup, then a third, tasting expertly.

CHAPTER 3

The eye of Tracy's tiger now and then wandered on the chance that it might behold a young lady tiger with appropriate manners for whatever might come of their seeing of one another, but almost never, when the tiger looked, did it see a young lady tiger. It was

young lady alley cats. On the few occasions when it did see a young
lady tiger Tracy's tiger was going somewhere in a hurry and had
time enough only to turn, still moving ahead, to look again. This
seemed a sad state of affairs, so the tiger said so.

"Lune," it said.

"What do you mean?" Tracy said.

"Alune."

"I don't get it."

"Ah lune."

"What's that?"

"Lunalune."

"Doesn't mean anything."

"Ah lunalune," the tiger said patiently.

"Speak English if you want to say something," Tracy said.

"La," the tiger said.

"That's almost French," Tracy said. "Speak English. You know I
don't know French."

"Sola."

"Solar?"

"So," the tiger said.

"Don't *shorten* the words," Tracy said, "lengthen them, so I can
figure out what you're trying to say."

"S," the tiger said.

"You can talk better than that," Tracy said. "Talk or shut up."

The tiger shut up.

Tracy considered what the tiger *had* said, and then suddenly it
came to him.

This happened during the lunch hour. Tracy was standing in the
sunlight on the steps of the entrance to Otto Seyfang's listening to
Nimmo, Peberdy, and Ringert talking about the eminence they had
achieved in the coffee world through faithful tasting. Every now
and then Tracy tried to get a word in edgewise about the song he
was writing, but he never quite made it.

He was trying to figure out what the tiger had said when a girl in
a tight-fitting yellow knit dress came walking down Warren Street.
She had a great deal of black hair combed straight down. There was
so much of it that it seemed to be a mane. It shined with life and

crackled with electricity. The muscles of Tracy's tiger became taut, its slim head pushed forward toward the girl, its tail shot straight out, rigid except for the almost imperceptible vibrating of it, and the tiger hummed low and violently, saying, "Eyeej."

The professional coffee tasters hearing the hum turned to Tracy in astonishment, for never before had they heard such an extraordinary sound.

"Oh," Tracy said to the tiger. "I get it."

"Eyeej," the tiger replied, as if in pain, its head moving out still farther, while Tracy's own eyes *dived* into the young lady's. The hum and the diving happened at the same time. The girl heard the hum, received the dive, almost stopped, almost smiled, pushed herself tighter against the yellow knit dress, and then danced on, the tiger moaning softly.

"Is that what they say in California?" Nimmo said.

"Eyeej," Tracy said.

"Say it again," Peberdy said.

Tracy, watching the girl go, watching the tiger lope after her, said it again.

"Hear that, Ringert?" Peberdy said. "That's what they say in California when they see a beauty."

"Don't worry," Ringert said. "I heard it."

"You *heard* it," Nimmo said, "but can you *do* it?"

"Of course I can't do it," Ringert said, "but neither can either of you old coffee tasters."

The coffee tasters agreed with regret that they could not do it, and then everybody went back to work, Tracy's tiger loping after Tracy to the piled sacks of coffee at the far end of the store room overlooking the alley. Tracy threw the sacks around all afternoon as if they were bean bags.

"Whoever she is," he said to the tiger, "she works around here somewhere. I'll see her tomorrow during the lunch hour, and the next day, too. The day after that I'll ask her to lunch."

Tracy talked to the tiger all afternoon, but all the tiger did was hum. Every now and then the other sack-throwers heard the hum. They were all young men, and they wanted to imitate the hum, but it was inimitable. You had to have a tiger. One of them, a man named Kalany, came near doing it, and boldly remarked to Tracy that anything anybody from California could do, *he* could do, being from Texas.

"Tomorrow, the next day, the day after," Tracy said to the tiger. "Then I'll ask her to lunch."

Sure enough, the schedule was met.

There she was across the table from Tracy at the O.K. Café, both of them eating, the tiger stalking around the table, trying not to hum or gulp.

"My name's Tom Tracy," Tracy said.

"I know," the girl said. "You told me."

"I forgot."

"I know. You told me three times. You mean Thomas of course, not Tom, don't you?"

"Yes," Tracy said. "Thomas Tracy. That's my name. That's all it is, I mean, that's just my name. A man's name isn't all there is to a man."

"Any middle name?" the girl said.

"No," Tracy said. "Just Thomas Tracy. Tom for short, if you want to shorten it."

"I don't want to," the girl said.

"No?" Tracy said, for this remark had great meaning for him. He was thrilled by the hope of the wonderful nature of this meaning. He was too thrilled to notice that the tiger was staring at something with so much excitement that its whole body was vibrating. He looked to see what it was that the tiger was staring at, and he saw that it was a young lady tiger.

"No?" Tracy said again.

"Yes," the girl said. "I like the name Thomas Tracy just as it is. Aren't you going to ask me *my* name?"

"What is it?" Tracy asked in a hushed voice.

"Laura Luthy," the girl said.

"Oh," Tracy moaned. "Oh, Laura Luthy."

"Do you like it?" Laura Luthy said.

"Do I *like* it?" Tracy said. "Oh, Laura, Laura Luthy."

The tigers chased around Laura Luthy and Thomas Tracy while they had lunch and they chased around them when they got up after lunch and walked to the cashier's where Tracy plunked down eighty-five cents for both lunches.

What did he care about money?

In the street Tracy took Laura's arm and walked past Otto Seyfang's, past Nimmo, Peberdy, and Ringert, standing out front. The two tigers walked sedately side by side. Tracy walked Laura to the office where she worked as a stenographer, two blocks down Warren Street near the docks.

"Tomorrow?" he said, not knowing what he meant but hoping *she* did.

"Yes," Laura said.

Tracy's tiger hummed. Laura's tiger half-smiled, hung its head, then turned away.

Tracy walked back to Otto Seyfang's, to the coffee tasters standing out front.

"Tracy," Nimmo said. "I hope I live long enough to see how this is going to turn out."

"You will," Tracy said. He spoke with anger and sincerity. "You'll live, Nimmo, because you've *got* to."

The tiger was now standing in the middle of the sidewalk staring into space.

On his way home after work that day Tracy found the tiger still standing in the middle of the sidewalk, and stood there himself, getting in the way of the after-work human traffic. He stood there beside the tiger a long time, then turned and began to walk to the subway, the tiger reluctantly following him.

CHAPTER 4

Laura Luthy lived in Far Rockaway. Saturdays and Sundays she stayed home with her mother.

Laura's mother, if anything, was more beautiful than Laura herself, so that there was a continuous if delicate rivalry between them in the mirrors around the house, and in their remarks about moving-picture actors, stage actors, men of the neighborhood, and men of the church. (The church was across the street, so that they were able to *see* who the men were. Saturdays and Sundays they watched together, but the rest of the time Laura's mother watched alone, or, being *free* to do so, didn't bother to do so. Now and then, though, it just happened that she saw a fine upright man enter the church late in the afternoon to confess, or collect a bill.)

This rivalry between mother and daughter enjoyed vigorous life in spite of the fact that Oliver Luthy, Laura's father, came home every night from work in Manhattan, and for twenty-four years had slept in the same bed with Mrs. Luthy, whose first name was Viola.

Mr. Luthy was in accounting. He had been in accounting as long as he'd been in the same bed, so to say, with Mrs. Luthy. It was she who had put him into it, expressing the opinion that it would be nicer if he were in something like accounting instead of in something like shipping, which was what he had been in when he had married her.

What he'd actually been was a shipping clerk, but Viola's way of putting it had always been that he was in shipping, for in putting it that way she often permitted herself to believe that it was cattle or tractors that he shipped, or perhaps *ships* themselves. She frequently believed that others got this fleeting impression, too, which she did not hasten to dispel. The impression seemed to dispel itself soon enough, anyway, but there was always that fleeting instant of daring if dubious glory.

Fine folk from nowhere in particular visited the Luthys quite frequently. There was something attractive about these visitors. They seemed to be, unlike the people one reads about in the society pages of newspapers, dirt. And yet, as their true selves became revealed—through the answering of kind questions asked by Viola—they seemed less and less to be dirt, and more and more as if, except for bad luck, they might have gone on the stage.

These visits were carefully planned, and generally fell on a Saturday afternoon. Once—no one knew but Viola herself—a man named Glear, stepping out of the bathroom into the hall and finding himself face to face with Viola, on her way back to the parlor from her bedroom with an old copy of the *Reader's Digest* in which she wished to show Mr. Glear an article about transportation, took her swiftly into his arms and did something to her face that was approximately a kiss. He smelled of Sen-Sen, she remembered, and had he gone into pictures would have been given office work to do—that is, in the pictures themselves. Knowing what she knew, knowing the effect she'd had on a dynamic man who might have been a film actor, she was rather difficult for Mr. Luthy for two years. By that time she had forgotten Mr. Glear's appearance and thought of him, not as Glear, but as Sherman, though God knows why.

"Whatever happened to that interesting man Sherman?" she once asked her husband, who replied that he had been made into a statue and placed in a park in Savannah.

Thomas Tracy himself visited the Luthys in Far Rockaway one Sunday afternoon.

The tiger had been tense during the entire journey to the Luthy house, impatient to see Laura's tiger again, and once Tracy and the tiger were inside the house extraordinary things began to happen.

Tracy noticed Laura's mother Viola, and Viola noticed Tracy. This noticing was not casual. It was understandable perhaps that Tracy *would* notice Viola, for there was a good deal about her that would have been impossible *not* to notice. She was all of Laura herself, not made larger by time, but more wicked by tiresome innocence.

Laura noticed this noticing that took place between Tracy and her mother, then noticed her father. *He* noticed that there was a great deal of action at the church across the street. Viola sent him for ice cream, which he was glad to fetch, for the church was on the way to the store, and he wanted to step in there to see what was going on.

When he was out of the house Viola brought a box of chocolates to Tracy and offered them to him with a considerable amount of implication. Laura, pretending to be glad that Tracy and her mother were getting on so well, asked to be excused a moment in order to see if she could find her penmanship certificate in which her name had been spelled Luty instead of Luthy.

Laura went off gaily, and there was Tracy and the tiger alone with Mrs. Luthy and the chocolates.

Tracy accepted a chocolate each time one was offered to him until he'd had six, whereupon, unable to account for it, he got up suddenly and accepted everything.

He was surprised to find that his acceptance was not unexpected, but rather anticipated. He, too, like Glear before him, grabbed the innocent woman and did something to her face that approximated a kiss. *His* breath smelled of teeth, Mrs. Luthy observed instantly.

Tracy stepped aside just in time to let the tiger go by, and then stepped aside again as the tiger came back, moving with fury. He then gave the theory of the kiss another go.

He was in the midst of this second effort when Laura Luthy returned to the room.

Tracy tried to pretend that what he was actually doing was *not* what it appeared to be, although he could not imagine anything like it at all that he could pretend it was instead.

He saw Laura's tiger standing beside Laura, glaring at him with astonishment and hate. He then looked for the other tiger, but it was gone.

Tracy took his hat and left the house.

He saw Mr. Luthy coming around the church with the ice cream, but he hurried away in the opposite direction.

It was not until he was back on Broadway, among the Sunday evening multitudes, that the tiger found its way through the people to walk beside him again.

"Don't ever do that again," Tracy said.

The next day during the lunch hour Tracy stood in front of Otto Seyfang's in the hope of seeing Laura Luthy, but she didn't come down the street.

It was the same every day of that week.

Chapter 5

"How's it turning out?" Nimmo asked Tracy on Friday at noon.

"The song?" Tracy said.

"No," Nimmo said. "Who cares about the song? How's it turning out with you and the black-haired beauty in the bright yellow dress?"

"Eyeej," Tracy said mournfully.

"What do you mean?" Nimmo said,

"I went to her house in Far Rockaway last Sunday and met her mother," Tracy said. "She brought out a box of chocolates, and I ate six of them. I hate chocolates, but she kept pushing the box in front of my face and I kept taking them and eating them. I'm afraid it's not turning out very well."

"Why?" Nimmo said.

"Well," Tracy said, "I'd had all those chocolates, the father had gone for ice cream, the daughter had gone for the penmanship certificate, I grabbed the mother and kissed her."

"No?" Nimmo said.

"Yes," Tracy said.

The coffee taster began to hiccup violently.

"What's the matter?" Tracy said.

"I don't know," Nimmo said.

"Maybe you'd better go home and lie down," Tracy said.

"No, I'm all right," Nimmo said. "Just tell me exactly what happened. I've got to know."

"Well," Tracy said. "It's like I said. I guess the chocolates made me crazy."

"What are you going to do?" Nimmo said.

"I'll make it turn out all right some way or another," Tracy said.

"How?"

"I'll be standing out here in front of Otto Seyfang's someday during my lunch hour," Tracy said, "and another girl something like Laura Luthy will come down Warren Street, and this time when I go out to her house and meet her mother I won't eat any chocolates, that's all."

"There isn't another girl *like* Laura Luthy, though," Nimmo said. "I guess I'll go in and taste some coffee."

"You've got twenty minutes more on your lunch hour," Tracy said.

"No, I'll go in now," Nimmo said. "What's the use standing out here? What's the use waiting any more?"

Nimmo was on his way in when he heard Tracy moan. He turned, and saw the black-haired beauty passing. But with her walked an unknown young man, obviously not from California, by appearance a bookkeeper.

Nimmo turned away in disgust, while Tracy stared in disbelief.

Tracy tried to smile but couldn't.

Laura Luthy passed by without even looking at him.

Nimmo couldn't stop hiccuping and was finally given the afternoon off. The following day he did not come to work. Monday morning Shively was in the Tasting Department at last, coming to work in his blue serge Sunday suit, for Nimmo was dead.

Some people say he died of the hiccups, but they are the kind of people who say Camille died of catarrh.

Chapter 6

What hearts have broken in times gone by, what hearts break now in our own times, what hearts shall break in times to come, Nimmo gone, Laura Luthy lost, Shively in the Tasting Department at last, Peberdy and Ringert treating him like a dog, frequently questioning his taste, looking at one another knowingly.

The three lines of Tracy's song turned out to be, as so many other things turn out to be, dirt. The song faded away, the very scrap of paper on which Tracy had so carefully written the words was lost, the melody was forgotten.

Tracy and the tiger walked one Sunday to Saint Patrick's on Fifth Avenue, burning with the fervor of an old and undefined religion that somehow seemed new, each of them walking in man's or animal's loneliness.

They went in and looked at everything.

The following Saturday Tracy quit his job at Otto Seyfang's and went back to San Francisco.

A number of years went by.

Then one day Tracy was twenty-seven, and he was back in New York, and he was walking there as he'd walked six years ago.

He turned off Broadway when he came to Warren Street and went down the street to Otto Seyfang's, which now bore the name of Keeney's Warehouse.

Did that mean coffee had failed, too? Nimmo, Peberdy, Ringert, Shively, Seyfang—had they all failed?

The tiger stiffened when it saw the entrance of the building, for it was there the tiger had stood one whole afternoon staring the way Laura Luthy had gone.

Tracy hurried away from Keeney's Warehouse, stopped a taxi, got in, and got out at the Public Library.

From there Tracy and the tiger began to walk up Fifth Avenue again. The street was full of Sunday people, men and women and their children.

Tracy had not yet found the one to take the place of Laura Luthy. Nimmo had predicted that Tracy would *never* find her, and perhaps Nimmo had been right, after all.

Tracy stood on a corner, a block from Saint Patrick's, and watched a small boy and the boy's sister cross the street. The tiger came up beside him. Tracy rested his hand on the tiger's head.

"They might have been mine," Tracy said.

"Eyeej," the tiger said.

Tracy strolled on, the tiger beside him. He was astonished to find that all of the people on his side of the street were moving swiftly to the other side of the street. He glanced at the other side of the street and saw people standing there, crowds of them, looking at him, some of them through cameras.

In all innocence Tracy decided to go across the street to find out what all the excitement was about, but when he stepped down from the curb to go, the people across the street began to run, some of them shouting, and a number of women screaming.

Tracy turned and looked at the tiger again.

Well, he'd had the tiger beside him most of his life, but never before had anything like this happened.

Never before had anybody else seen the tiger.

Was it possible now that the tiger was actually being seen by others, by everybody?

A number of dogs on leashes began to yap and bark and carry on. This also was something new. Tracy stopped in the middle of Fifth Avenue to let a bus go by, and was astonished once again, this time by the face of the driver of the bus, and by the faces of the passengers.

"Well, what do you know?" Tracy said to the tiger. "I believe they can see you. I believe they can actually see you, just as I've seen you most of my life, but look at them, they're terrified, they're scared to death. Good God, they ought to know there's nothing to be afraid of."

"Eyeej," the tiger said.

"Yes," Tracy said. "I haven't heard you speak so well since we were at Otto Seyfang's and Laura Luthy came dancing down Warren Street."

Tracy and the tiger moved up Fifth Avenue until they were across the street from Saint Patrick's. Tracy had planned to go into the church, as he and the tiger had done six years ago, and so he began to cross the street, to get to the church, but as he did so the few people in front of the church broke and ran. And then everybody in the church came out. Tracy and the tiger were late for church, but even so, they would go in, and Tracy would walk all the way down the centre aisle with the tiger and look again at all the fine things there, the wonderful height and light, the stained-glass windows, the fine pillars, the burning candles.

The people who came out of the church seemed at peace, and then suddenly they deteriorated, some of them running down side streets, some up and down Fifth Avenue, and some back into the church, to hide there.

"I'm awful sorry about this," Tracy said. "It's never happened before, as you know."

"Eyeej," the tiger said.

"We're going to church anyway," Tracy said.

He rested his hand on the tiger's head, and thus they went together to the steps of the church, up the steps, and then on to the handsome area that was inside.

But if the *area* was handsome, the people still in the area were not, including several men in robes. Their going was swift and untidy.

Tracy and the tiger walked slowly down the center aisle. He noticed shut doors here and there opening a little, frightened eyes staring out at him, and he saw the doors shut again, heard them being locked or bolted.

"Well, it *is* a beautiful place," Tracy said, "but you remember how different it was when we came here six years ago. The place was full of people then, men, women, and children, and they were all glad about something, not the way they are now, scared to death, gone running, or hiding behind doors. What are they afraid of? What's happened to them?"

"Eyeej," the tiger said.

Tracy and the tiger left the church by a side door that opened on 50th Street, but when they came to the street Tracy saw an armoured car standing there, with gun barrels pointed at him and the tiger.

He looked down the street, and there near Madison Avenue he saw
another armoured car. He looked up to Fifth Avenue, and there on
the corner he saw two more of them. Beyond the armoured cars was
a multitude of people, all terrified, waiting for a fight of some kind,
and an outcome.

The man who sat in the driver's seat of the armoured car directly
in front of Tracy quickly raised the window of the car, to be better
protected against the tiger.

"What's the matter?" Tracy said.

"For God's sake man," the driver replied, "don't you see the animal beside you?"

"Of course I see it," Tracy said.

"It's a panther escaped from the circus," the driver said.

"Don't be silly," Tracy said. "It's never been *near* the circus. And
it's *not* a panther, it's a tiger."

"Stand aside, man," the driver said, "so one of the men can shoot
the animal."

"Shoot it?" Tracy said. "Are you crazy?"

He began to walk down 50th Street toward Madison Avenue. The
driver of the armoured car started the motor, and the car moved
slowly beside Tracy, the driver trying to argue him into stepping
away from the tiger.

"Stand aside, man," the driver said.

"Go on," Tracy said. "Take your armoured car back to the bank
or the garage or wherever it is you keep it."

"Stand back or we'll shoot anyway," the driver said.

"You wouldn't dare," Tracy said.

"O.K., boy," the driver said. "You asked for it."

Tracy heard the shot. He looked to see if the tiger had been hit. It
hadn't, but it *was* off for Madison Avenue.

The tiger was swift, swifter than Tracy had ever before known it
to be. When it reached the second armoured car on 50th Street
another shot was fired, the tiger leaped, fell, and when it began to
run again Tracy noticed that it did so with the right front foot held
up. When the tiger reached Madison Avenue, it turned uptown, and
disappeared, the nearest armoured car going after it with all of its
slow might.

Tracy broke into a trot, chasing after the tiger.

He was stopped at the corner by three officers. They pushed him into the second armoured car and drove off with him.

"What do you want to kill my tiger for?" Tracy said to the driver.

"That animal escaped from the circus last night, after mauling a keeper," the driver said.

"What are you talking about?" Tracy said.

"You heard me," the man said.

"I've had that tiger most of my life," Tracy said.

"You haven't had *any* tiger most of your life," the driver said, "but you've had *something*, and we'll soon find out what it is."

CHAPTER 7

Tracy sat in a Bank of England chair at the center of an enormous room in which newspapermen, photographers, police officers, animal trainers, and a good many others milled about.

If the tiger had actually not been his own tiger, as they said, his own tiger was certainly not with Tracy now.

He sat alone.

The tiger did not sit on the floor at his feet.

Tracy had been in the chair more than an hour.

Somebody new came into the room suddenly.

"Dr. Pingitzer," Tracy heard somebody say.

This was a small, smiling man of seventy or so.

"Now," the man said quickly to the crowd. "What is it?"

The doctor was drawn to one side and surrounded by a group of experts, several of whom told him what it was.

"Ah ha," Tracy heard the doctor say. The doctor went quickly to Tracy.

"My boy," he said. "I am Rudolph Pingitzer."

Tracy got up and shook Rudolph Pingitzer's hand.

"Thomas Tracy," he said.

"Ah ha, Thomas Tracy," Dr. Pingitzer turned to the others. "Perhaps a chair like this for *me*, too?"

Another Bank of England chair was quickly fetched for the doctor.

He sat down and said pleasantly, "I am seventy-two years old."

"I am twenty-seven," Tracy said.

Dr. Pingitzer filled a pipe, spilled a good deal of tobacco over his clothing which he did not bother to brush off, used seven matches to get the pipe lighted, puffed at it a dozen times, then said with the pipe in his mouth, "I have wife, sixty-nine years old, boy forty-five years old, psychiatrist, boy forty-two years old, psychiatrist, boy thirty-nine years old, psychiatrist, girl thirty-six years old, says *thirty-one* years old, psychiatrist, girl thirty-one years old, says *twenty-six* years old, psychiatrist, furnished apartment, phonograph, piano, television, typewriter, but with typewriter I have mechanical disorder."

"Why don't you get it fixed?" Tracy said.

"Ah, yes," Dr. Pingitzer said. "Never use typewriter. Is for grandchildren. Junk. I have these things, mostly psychiatrist."

"Do you have any money?" Tracy said.

"No," Dr. Pingitzer said. "Is expensive so many psychiatrists. Have books. Have also, ah, yes, bed. For sleep. At night. I lie down. Sleep. Is change."

"Do you have any friends?" Tracy said.

"Many friends," Dr. Pingitzer said. "Of course when I say friends"—Dr. Pingitzer's hands moved quickly, he made odd little noises—"you understand I mean"—more noises—"naturally. Who knows?"

"Do you go to church?" Tracy said.

"Ah," Dr. Pingitzer said. "Yes. Sentiment. I like it. It is nice."

A newspaperman stepped forward, and said "How about *you* asking the questions, doctor?"

"Ah ha?" the doctor said quickly. "If to be interview with Dr. Pingitzer room to be empty."

A police captain who was in charge, a man named Huzinga, said quickly, "O.K., you heard the doctor. Everybody out."

There was a good deal of protesting on the part of the newspapermen, but Huzinga and his men got everybody out into the hall. When the room was empty, the doctor, puffing on his pipe peacefully, smiled at Tracy, then began to doze. Tracy himself was tired by now, so he began to doze, too. The old man snored, but Tracy didn't.

After a moment the door was pushed open, and a photographer quickly took a picture of the men asleep in the Bank of England chairs.

Huzinga then came in and woke the doctor up.

"Ah ha," the doctor said.

Huzinga was about to wake Tracy up, too, but the doctor said, "No. Important."

"Yes, doctor," Huzinga said.

He tiptoed out of the room.

The little man sat and watched Tracy's face. After a moment Tracy opened his eyes.

"I dream I was in Vienna," the doctor said.

"When were you there last?" Tracy said,

"Twenty years ago," Dr. Pingitzer said. "Long, long ago. I like very much ice cream. Vanilla."

"Do you like coffee?" Tracy said.

"Coffee?" Dr. Pingitzer said. "I am from Vienna. I *live* on coffee. Ah ha." He shouted, so that they would hear him beyond the door. "Coffee, please!"

Outside, Huzinga sent an officer for a pot of coffee and two cups.

"He knows," Huzinga said to the officer. "He knows what he's doing."

"We will have coffee," the little man said. "Is happened something. I don't know."

"They shot my tiger," Tracy said.

"I am sorry," Dr. Pingitzer said.

"We went into Saint Patrick's," Tracy said, "just as we did six years ago, but when we came out they were waiting there in an armoured car, and another one farther down on 50th Street. The first shot went wild, but it frightened the tiger, and it began to run. When it reached the second armoured car the tiger was shot in the foot."

"This tiger, it is *your* tiger?"

"Yes."

"Why?"

"It's been with me most of my life."

"Ah," the little man said. "It is tiger, like dog is dog?"

"Do you mean," Tracy said, "is it a *real* tiger, as a tiger in the jungle is, or in the circus?"

"Precise," Dr. Pingitzer said.

"No, it is not," Tracy said. "It wasn't until today, at any rate, but it was real today. It was still *my* tiger, though."

"Why do they say tiger is escape from circus?"

"I don't know."

"Is possible?"

"I suppose so. A caged animal of any kind might escape from a circus, if possible."

"You are not afraid of this tiger?" Dr. Pingitzer said. "We have here someplace photographs taken by newspaper photographers. My young daughter have hobby of photography one time. Pictures, pictures, pictures of Papa. *Me!*" He turned to the door and spoke loudly. "Photographs, please."

Huzinga came in, and off the top of a desk picked up a dozen photographs, handed them to the doctor, who quickly ran through them, with scarcely time enough to look at any of them, his hands and eyes moving extraordinarily swiftly.

"You are not afraid of this animal," he said again quickly, "this tiger. This is *black panther.*"

"Yes, I know," Tracy said, "but it's my tiger just the same."

"You have this name *tiger* for this animal?"

"Yes, I know it's a black panther," Tracy said, "but I've always thought of it as a tiger."

"*Your* tiger?"

"Yes."

"You are not afraid of this tiger?"

"No."

"Everybody is afraid of tiger."

"Everybody is afraid of many things," Tracy said.

"I am afraid of night," Dr. Pingitzer said. "In Vienna at night I go as a young man where are many lights, much brightness. That way I am not afraid of night."

The coffee was brought in and poured by Huzinga, who seemed, for some reason, worshipful of Dr. Pingitzer.

"Now, we taste coffee," the doctor said.

"I wanted to be a coffee taster once," Tracy said.

"Ah, yes?" Dr. Pingitzer said. "Let us drink coffee now. Enjoy coffee. Life is too short." He waved at the door. "Much—much— much——" He made a face, and was unable to finish the thought.

"Yes," Tracy said.

They drank coffee in silence, Tracy tasting it carefully, as he had done six years ago at Otto Seyfang's, sitting with Nimmo, Peberdy, and Ringert.

CHAPTER 8

After they had tasted three cups each Dr. Pingitzer said, "Ah ha. Work. I hate work. I hate psychiatry. I *always* hate work. I like fun, play, imagination, magic."

"Why do you work, then?" Tracy said.

"Why?" Dr. Pingitzer said. "Confusion." The doctor reflected a moment. "In Vienna I see this girl. Elsa. This is Elsa Varshock. Ah ha. Elsa is wife, is mother, is say, 'Where's for food, money?' So? I work."

"You understand psychiatry?" Tracy said.

"Psychiatry, no," Dr. Pingitzer said. "People—little bit. Little, little, little bit. Every year, every day—less, less, less. Why? People is difficult. People is people. People is fun, play, imagination, magic. Ah ha. People is pain, people is sick, people is mad, people is hurt, people is hurt *people,* is kill, is kill self. Where is fun, where is play, where is imagination, where is magic? Psychiatry I hate. People I love. Mad people, beautiful people, hurt people, sick people, broke people, in pieces people, I love, I love. Why? Why is lost from people fun, play, imagination, magic? What for? Ah ha. Money?" He smiled. "I think so. Money. Is love, this money. Is beauty, this money. Is fun, this money. Where is money? I do not know. No more fun. Work, now. Work. Tiger. Tiger."

"Do you know the poem?" Tracy said.

"*Is poem?*" Dr. Pingitzer said.

"Of course."

"What is this poem?" Dr. Pingitzer said.

>*"Tiger! Tiger! burning bright,"* Tracy said.
>*"In the forests of the night,*
>*What immortal hand or eye*
>*Could frame thy fearful symmetry?"*

"Ah ha. Is more?" Dr. Pingitzer said.

"Yes, quite a bit," Tracy said, "if I haven't forgotten it."

"Please," Dr. Pingitzer said.

"In what distant deeps or skies," Tracy went on.
"Burnt the fire of thine eyes?
On what wings dare he aspire?
What the hand dare seize the fire?"

"Ho ho," Dr. Pingitzer said. "Is poem like *this* I do not hear seventy-two years! Who do this poem?"

"William Blake," Tracy said.

"Bravo, William Blake!" Dr. Pingitzer said.

"Is more?"

"Yes," Tracy said. "Let me see. Oh yes,

> *"And what shoulder, and what art,*
> *Could twist the sinews of thy heart?*
> *And when thy heart began to beat,*
> *What dread hand? and what dread feet?"*

"More?" the doctor said.

"I think I've got it all now," Tracy said.

> *"What the hammer? What the chain?*
> *In what furnace was thy brain?*
> *What the anvil? What dread grasp*
> *Dare its deadly terrors clasp?*
>
> *"When the stars threw down their spears,*
> *And watered heaven with their tears,*
> *Did He smile His work to see?*
> *Did He who made the Lamb make thee?*
>
> *"Tiger! Tiger! burning bright*
> *In the forests of the night,*
> *What immortal hand or eye,*
> *Dare frame thy fearful symmetry?"*

Tracy stopped. "That's the whole poem," he said.

"Ah, ha," Dr. Pingitzer said. "Thank you. Now, you have this poem since childhood. Yes?"

"Yes," Tracy said. "I began to recite it when I was three."

"You *understand* this poem?" Dr. Pingitzer said.

"I don't *understand* anything," Tracy said. "I *like* this poem."

"Ah ha. True."

The old man turned to the door.

"Much—much—much—" he said. "Now. Two questions. One. Your tiger, is *what*?"

"Mine," Tracy said.

"Two," Dr. Pingitzer said. "Tiger in street, is *what*?"

"Well," Tracy said, "I suppose a black panther mauled a keeper and escaped from the circus last night. Such things happen. I suppose a wounded black panther is now loose in New York. I suppose it will, out of fear, kill somebody if it thinks it must. But the black panther that is loose in the city is *also* my tiger."

"So?"

"Yes."

"Why?" Dr. Pingitzer said.

"I don't know," Tracy said, "but it walked up Fifth Avenue with me and into Saint Patrick's. It didn't attack anybody. It stayed beside me. It didn't run until it was shot at. Wouldn't *you* run if you were shot at?"

"Very fast," Dr. Pingitzer said. "Seventy-two, but very fast." He paused a moment, to imagine himself running very fast at seventy-two.

"The police, they will kill this animal," Dr. Pingitzer said.

"They'll *try* to," Tracy said.

"They *will*."

"They'll *try*," Tracy said, "but they won't, because they can't."

"Why? They can't?" Dr. Pingitzer said.

"The tiger can't be killed."

"One tiger? Can't be killed? Why not?"

"It can't, that's all," Tracy said

"But *tiger* will kill?" Dr. Pingitzer said.

"If it must," Tracy said.

"Is this right?"

"I don't know. Is it?"

"I also don't know," the doctor said. "I know very little. Very, very, very little. Ah ha. Question of psychiatry. You are mad?"

"Yes, of course," Tracy said. The old man looked toward the door. He put a finger to his lips.

"Soft," he whispered.

"I'm mad because they wounded the tiger," Tracy said. "I'm mad because they put the tiger in the cage in the first place. I'm mad because they put it in the circus. But I am also mad, from birth."

"I, also, but this is information *not* to say," Dr. Pingitzer said. He looked at the door again. He got up suddenly. "I speak so. *This man is sane.* This they understand. Ah ha! Work finish." He called out loudly. "O.K., please."

Huzinga was the first to enter the room, but soon everybody was back in.

Dr. Pingitzer surveyed the faces, waited a long time for silence, then said, "Ah ha! This man is sane."

A man altogether unlike Dr. Pingitzer stepped forward and said, "Dr. Pingitzer, I am Dr. Scatter, in charge of Neuro, Borough of Manhattan. May I ask the psychiatric course by which you have reached your conclusion?"

"No," Dr. Pingitzer said. He turned to Tracy. "Good-bye, my boy," he said.

"Good-bye," Tracy said.

Dr. Pingitzer glanced at everyone in the room, then went to the door.

On his way he was photographed by a number of newspaper photographers, one of whom said, "Dr. Pingitzer, how about the black panther? Is it *his,* as he said it is?"

"I have examine *him,* not black panther," the doctor said.

A reporter stepped up to Dr. Pingitzer.

"How did it happen that the black panther didn't harm him, doctor?" the reporter said.

"I don't know," Dr. Pingitzer said.

"Well, what have you found out about it, after talking to him?" the reporter said.

"Nothing," the doctor said.

"What about a black panther being loose in the city?" the reporter said.

"This is not psychiatry problem," the doctor said.

"What kind of a problem is it?" the reporter said.

"Where from is this black panther?"

"From the circus."

"Circus problem," Dr. Pingitzer said. He walked out of the room.

Everybody gathered around Dr. Scatter, who was not at all satisfied with Dr. Pingitzer's conclusion, or manners.

CHAPTER 9

Tracy, in walking with the tiger, had broken no law.

Still, what he *had* done seemed so enormous and unbelievable as to *seem* illegal, or at any rate arrogant, thoughtless, and rude.

At the very least, it was felt, he must be insane. A man just naturally doesn't walk with a black panther escaped from the circus as if the animal and he were on terms of perfect understanding.

Therefore, after the departure of Dr. Pingitzer, Tracy was examined by Dr. Scatter, who found it irresistible to interpret Tracy's replies in a manner convenient to his education and prejudices.

Dr. Scatter had no difficulty in proving, step by step, that Tracy was in fact mad. This is easy to do. It can be done with anybody.

"Futhermore," Dr. Scatter said to the others involved, including Police Captain Earl Huzinga, who was the only one in the group who maintained disbelief in Dr. Scatter's findings and persisted in being respectful of Dr. Pingitzer's, "when the subject was asked what his reaction would be to an indefinite visit at Bellevue for the purpose of more prolonged and thorough psychiatric investigation, he replied that he would rather go home but that if forced to go to Bellevue he would make the most of his visit and feel just as much at home there as anywhere else, if not more at home. This attitude suggests that, in addition to all the other symptoms already identified, the subject has a martyr complex. It also reveals psychotic arrogance, and contempt for the collective intelligence. The subject is obviously deluded, believing that he is personally exempted from the laws which guide and control the rest of society. This belief is based upon, and has been strengthened by, a prolonged association with a fantasy tiger, which he declares is his, and his alone; which he has confessed is capable of speech—that is, communication by speech with *himself alone*. I am sure there is no doubt in anyone's mind that he must be placed in Bellevue for observation and treatment."

Thus, Thomas Tracy, on a pleasant Sunday afternoon in October, was placed in Bellevue.

He found the people there quite mad. He also found that each of them had a tiger: a very troubled one, a very angry one, a most deeply wounded one, a tiger deprived of humor, and love of freedom and fun, imagination, and hope.

Nimmo's son was there with a depressed and dying tiger. Peberdy's daughter was there with a terrified tiger that paced back and forth. Ringert himself was there with a tiger that resembled a weary old dog.

And Laura Luthy was there, her once magnificent tiger now thin, starved, and pathetic....

Only Tracy was without a tiger.

Tracy's tiger was hiding under the establishment of Roush, Rubeling and Ryan on Madison Avenue between 55th and 56th. The place was dark, secret, and deathly. The tiger was in hiding under the room in which Roush, Rubeling, and Ryan decorated the dead with powder, rouge, and smiles.

The tiger lay there in terror and loneliness, bereaved, heartsick, and eager itself to be dead.

CHAPTER 10

What's the use trying to describe the effect upon the people of New York of the story of Tracy and the tiger, as reported on the front pages of every newspaper, as told by anonymous and famous newscasters of radio and television, as embellished by newsreels of Tracy and the tiger walking up Fifth Avenue, entering Saint Patrick's, coming out of Saint Patrick's? As further embellished by photographs of Tracy drinking coffee with Dr. Pingitzer, surrounded by police, newspaper reporters, psychiatrists, others?

The effect was the usual one.

Innocent dogs, on their way to relief, came upon men who dropped dead, women screamed at shadows, then slapped their children for wanting to go out and play.

Everybody stayed home Sunday night, and quite a few Monday morning, for the tiger was still at large, and Tracy was in Bellevue.

He was examined a good deal of the time.

He in turn found his examiners interesting.

In his spare time Tracy visited Laura Luthy, who could not remember him. He brought up the matter of the Sunday visit in Far Rockaway, but Laura, pale and wan now, did not remember.

"I ate six soft chocolates," Tracy said.

"You should have had seven," Laura said.

"Why?"

"Then you would have had one extra," Laura said. "One extra is always nice. I have always believed that. One extra for everybody."

"Chocolates?" Tracy said.

"Anything," Laura said. "Mother, father, life, chance. Six is fine, but one extra makes it finer. Another and another, you should have had another."

"Don't you remember?" Tracy said. "Your father went for ice cream."

"Ice cream melts," Laura said. "That is the secret of ice cream. It melts."

"Laura," Tracy said. "Look at me. Listen to me."

"Nothing is so sad as ice cream melting," Laura said.

"It's not sad, Laura," Tracy said. "Ice cream's *supposed* to melt."

"It is?"

"Of course."

"I didn't know," Laura said. "I cried so hard when I saw the ice cream melt."

"What ice cream, Laura?"

"The ice cream girl, the ice cream boy," Laura said. "I didn't know. All those tears for nothing. I cried until I melted, too. Are you sure?"

"No," Tracy said. "No, I'm not sure. I don't know what happened, but whatever it was, listen to me, Laura. Six years ago I was standing in front of Otto Seyfang's."

"Why were you standing *there*?" Laura said.

"I *worked* there," Tracy said. "I was standing there talking to the coffee tasters, Nimmo, Peberdy, and Ringert."

"Where are they now?" Laura said.

"Nimmo's dead," Tracy said. "Ringert's here, and I don't know where Peberdy is. While I was standing there a beautiful girl came down Warren Street."

"*Was* she beautiful?" Laura said.

"The most beautiful girl in the world."

"Who was she?"

"You, Laura," Tracy said.

"Me?" Laura said. "The most beautiful girl in the world? You must be mistaken."

"No. It *was* you, Laura."

"Well, I'm certainly not the most beautiful girl in the world any more," Laura said.

"That's what I want to talk about," Tracy said.

"All right," Laura said. "Talk about it."

"I want *you* to come down Warren Street again."

"You do?"

"Yes."

"Why?"

"Well, I don't know how else to put it," Tracy said. "I love you."

"What do you mean?" Laura said.

"I don't know," Tracy said.

"I suppose I mean—you're still the most beautiful girl in the world."

"I'm not," Laura said.

"Yes, you are," Tracy said. "You are to *me*."

"No," Laura said. "It's so arrogant to be beautiful. It's such bad taste. It's so pathetic, too. So much more pathetic than just lying still and knowing you're dead."

"You're not dead, Laura."

"Oh, I am."

"Laura!" Tracy said. "For God's sake, Laura, I love you."

"I'm sorry," Laura said. "I'm terribly sorry. I think I prefer to be dead."

Tracy didn't know what to think. Was she *actually* mad?

Like Dr. Pingitzer, he didn't know.

She was at Bellevue, at any rate.

She'd had a high fever for months.

The opinion of the experts was that she would soon be dead.

Later on, they knew, they too would be dead, but this did not trouble them because they believed they might die sane.

CHAPTER 11

A hectic week for New York went by. The tiger was still at large. That is to say, it was dying of starvation and fear under the embalming room of Roush, Rubeling and Ryan. According to the newspapers, however, on Monday morning the tiger was seen in three different places in Harlem, two in Greenwich Village, six in Brooklyn, and a boy in Fresno, California, killed a black cat with a .22 rifle because it looked enough like Tracy's tiger to make it worth his while. A photograph of the boy, proudly holding the cat by the tail, appeared in newspapers all over the country.

His name was Benintendi, first name Salvatore.

By sundown Tuesday Tracy's Tiger, as it was now called, was seen by miscellaneous people all over the country.

A man in London saw it in Soho and explained in a letter to *The Times* how the creature, as he called it, had reached there. His explanation was quite interesting, and his sympathies were entirely with the creature, as British sympathies sometimes are, at least among her gentle eccentrics.

A bookie in Seattle who had been beaten by a rival bookie's thugs informed the police that he had been attacked by Tracy's Tiger.

A saloon-keeper in Chicago advertised a new drink called Tracy's Tiger, twenty-five cents a shot.

A toy manufacturer in Toledo called in his designers and salesmen, and by Saturday morning had a black velvet Tracy's Tiger for children to take to bed. He also had a sweater on which was stamped a picture of the animal and its name, all sizes of Tracy's Tiger made of inflated rubber, and a jack-in-the-box out of which Tracy's Tiger sprang at one's loved ones.

The animal itself had a cold that was quickly turning to pleurisy. Its eyes were lustreless. They were giving off a good deal of yellow mucus. Its nose was clogged. Its white teeth had become coated with something that tasted like the end.

The observing of Tracy continued, and was dutifully reported to the nation and the world every day, along with other, equally peculiar, news.

A dozen or more reputations were made by psychiatrists and newspapermen on Tracy and his Tiger.

Tracy's devotion to Laura Luthy was discovered by an astute newspaperman who scooped the world with a story captioned

TRACY LOVES LAURA

TIGER BOY WOOS BELLEVUE BELLE

The *Mirror*, however, having had poor luck in its photographs and stories about Tracy and the tiger, got even with the other newspapers by demanding an instantaneous investigation of the city's police, and if need be the dismissal of Chief August Bly, for if he could not kill or capture a lame tiger, how would he take care of the citizens of New York in the event a bomb was dropped on the city?

This theme was taken up by a number of people who readily take up miscellaneous themes.

Chief Bly was asked point-blank by the *Mirror*, "When can you assure the people of the greatest city in the world that Tracy's Tiger will be killed or captured, and permit the people to sleep peacefully again?"

The question was asked by telegram.

Chief Bly called in his brightest men and asked them to answer the telegram. There were a dozen different answers, all unsatisfactory, because nobody *knew* when the tiger would be killed or captured.

"I don't know," the Chief wanted to say but didn't dare.

Instead, a 500-word reply was written and dispatched by telegram to the *Mirror*. The reply was run on the front page of the *Mirror* under the heading of *Shame on the New York Police*. The *Mirror* demanded that Chief Bly resign. It also offered a reward of $5,000 to any man, woman, or child, regardless of race, color, creed, or religion, who brought Tracy's Tiger to the *Mirror*, dead or alive.

The following day a man went to the *Mirror* with a black panther shot through the head, and the *Mirror* had the scoop it wanted at last.

The stories and photographs of the killing of Tracy's Tiger were sent all over the country and all over the world.

The man, Art Pliley, in a matter of hours received hundreds of 'phone calls at the *Mirror*, mostly from women, several of whom offered to be his bride. Negotiations were under way for him to buy a clean suit and appear in a Men of Distinction advertisement when the police escorted Tracy to the *Mirror* to have a look at the tiger.

Each of the other papers had a reporter and a photographer on hand, just in case. It seemed a wild and pathetic chance for the Chief of Police to be taking, but it was worth looking into just the same.

The *Mirror,* however, refused to permit Tracy to examine the tiger.

Art Pliley was asked to shake hands with Tracy for a photograph, but by now he knew the ropes, and said, "I couldn't do that for less than five."

"Five what?" he was asked.

"Hundred," Art Pliley said. "The *Mirror* can photograph me for nothing. That's in my contract. Any other paper, though, five."

"This is a high school paper," the photographer said as a joke, and Art Pliley, never having attended high school and believing it was his duty, shook hands with Tracy free of charge.

He was given a severe bawling out by the managing editor of the *Mirror,* however.

As for Tracy, he shook hands with everybody. He believed they were sincere. Either that, or helpless.

The *News* charged that the *Mirror* had perpetrated a hoax on the citizens of New York, and that the dead tiger in their possession was not Tracy's Tiger.

The upshot of this rivalry and jealousy resulted after two days in a formal and ceremonious examination of the *Mirror's* tiger by Tracy, by the animal's trainer at the circus, and by a half-dozen people who wanted any kind of publicity they could possibly get.

The ceremony was swift. Tracy looked at the poor dead black panther lying beside the specially built casket in which the *Mirror* planned to bury it. He looked, that is, from across the room. He spoke altogether out of turn, too, making a shambles of the whole ceremony.

"That's not my tiger," he said. "That's not even a black panther. That's a mountain lion that's had its fur dyed black."

Art Pliley, to sum up the hoax, was arrested, his bank account confiscated by the *Mirror,* and he was put in jail. There he was visited by the managing editor of the *News,* however, and a new deal was made. If Pliley would confess exclusively to the *News,* the *News* would give him *six* thousand dollars. Pliley confessed every day for three days, whereupon he was sent to the penitentiary, for in confessing, he was thorough, and revealed that he had a good many other clever things. He said he'd always wanted to be famous mainly, and since he *was* famous at last, he didn't want to stop half-way.

It would be tedious to go into the nature of his confessions. He wanted to be famous, that's all.

Tracy's Tiger grew very ill on the ninth day of hiding under the embalming room of Roush, Rubeling and Ryan. That night, in trembling desperation, it crawled out from its hiding place to an open garbage can in which it found meat scraps, bones, and outer leaves of miscellaneous vegetables. Much of this scrap it carried to its hiding place, making one trip after another.

A small boy, awake at two in the morning, coughing and waiting for his mother to bring him the cough medicine, said to her when she came with it, "Look at the big cat in the garbage can, Mama."

Mama looked and woke up Papa. Papa had no gun, but he *was* an amateur photographer, and he *did* have a flash camera.

Papa sat at the window three minutes, waiting for the tiger to come back to the garbage can. When the tiger came back Papa got something like buck fever, and found that he couldn't snap the picture.

Mama took the camera angrily out of his hands and handed it to the boy, eight years old. The boy focused as well as he was able to, the tiger saw the flash, leaped, and went back to its hiding place.

The man put on his clothes and developed the picture in his own dark-room. The picture showed the rear half of the tiger.

The man went to the police with the picture of the rear half of Tracy's Tiger. The police questioned the man an hour, and at four that morning the sick tiger heard voices and saw lights. It watched and listened a long time.

When things quieted down, the tiger came out and began to move downtown.

The photograph, and the story of its achievement, was duly published in the newspapers, along with photographs of the sick boy, who immediately grew sicker.

The area of New York in which the boy lived was drawn by special map-makers, and speculations were made as to where the tiger was now hiding.

Chapter 12

Police Captain Earl Huzinga, after many quiet chats with Tracy at
Bellevue, made up his mind to go directly to Chief Bly and say his
piece, even if it cost him his job.

"He can get us the tiger," Captain Huzinga said.

"How?" Chief Bly said.

"Well, it *sounds* complicated," Huzinga said, "but I've had a lot of
talks with him, and it's not complicated. I know he can do it."

"How?" Bly said again.

"First," Huzinga said, "he doesn't want anybody to know about
it. No publicity at all."

"We can keep it quiet," the Chief said. He was sick and tired of
the whole thing and beginning to feel older than his sixty-six years.

"There's a place on Warren Street that used to be Otto Seyfang's,
a coffee importing house," Huzinga said. "It's out of business now,
but the building's still there. It's a warehouse now. Tracy wants a sign
made like the old sign, *Otto Seyfang's,* and he wants the sign put up
where it was. He wants the Tasting Department restored, and he
wants a man named Peberdy, a man named Ringert, and a man named
Shively to sit there and taste coffee. Peberdy's living in a furnished
room. Ringert's at Bellevue. Shively's living with his daughter in
the Bronx."

"What's he want all this nonsense for?" Bly said.

"I know it doesn't sound reasonable," Huzinga said, "but I know
he'll get us the tiger. He needs only one day. It's got to be a Sunday.
That suits us fine because there won't be anybody but one or two
drunks on Warren Street at noon on a Sunday,"

"You've been at Bellevue so long," Chief Bly said, "you've gone a
little bats yourself, but go on, let's hear the whole thing."

"He wants at least a hundred sacks of coffee in the storeroom,"
Huzinga said.

"What for?"

"He used to work there," Huzinga said. "On this Sunday he's going
to get there at eight in the morning. He's going to lift and carry the
sacks. Peberdy, Ringert, and Shively will be in the Tasting Department tasting coffee. Every now and then Tracy will stop carrying
sacks, and go in there and taste some coffee with them. At noon he'll

stop work, go out front, and stand there in the sun. At half-past twelve a girl named Laura Luthy will come walking down Warren Street. She'll stop in front of Otto Seyfang's."

"She will?" Bly said.

"Yes," Huzinga said.

"So what?" Bly said.

"In a moment Tracy's Tiger will be there, too," Huzinga said. "He'll take the girl by the arm and walk down Warren Street with her. There's an empty store three doors down from Otto Seyfang's—used to be a produce house. He'll walk into this store with the girl and the tiger. In the store will be a cage. The tiger will go into the cage. Tracy will lock the cage. Then, he and the girl will walk out of the store."

"He will?"

"Yes."

"Go ahead," the Chief said. "Tell me more."

"Two things we've got to promise him" Huzinga said. "*One.* Absolutely no publicity. No photographs, not even for our own records. You and I can watch from the building across the street. *Two.* We can *have* the tiger in the cage, but we have got to promise that we do not announce to anybody that we've got it. If the tiger's ill, we've got to give it expert care, especially the injured foot. It's the right front one."

"You believe this nut, don't you?" Chief Bly said.

"Yes, sir."

"You put me on the case ten days ago," Huzinga said. "I've been with him the entire time. That was no bull in the papers about Laura Luthy. The doctors said she was dying, and all you had to do was see her to *know* she was. Well, she's not dying anymore. Pingitzer's in there every day talking with both of them, trying to figure it out. He says everybody at Bellevue is somebody who lost love somewhere along the line. The ones that love means the most to get sick, a lot of them die. It doesn't take very long, either. Tracy's not crazy."

"What about Dr. Scatter and all the other experts who say he *is* crazy?" the Chief said.

"I don't know," Huzinga said. "Their reports seem to stack up all right. I guess there are a couple of ways of looking at things like that, though. Pingitzer's studying Tracy's way. He says it's a way he's always *believed* might work, especially if it's started early enough, but he's never seen it work in an advanced case like Laura Luthy's. He says when it comes to human beings, you've got to be patient, you've got to be willing to learn, because anything can happen, especially if love's involved. You wouldn't think there'd be laughter in Bellevue, would you?"

"No, I wouldn't, not decent laughter anyway," Bly said.

"Well, there is, and it's *damned* decent," Huzinga said. "Scatter and all the others are getting annoyed by it, too. They're trying to stop it. They're bringing out new regulations every day, but they can't stop it. They're sore because the patients aren't acting the way they're *supposed* to act. They get up, visit one another, help one another, tell stories, dance, sing—and I don't mean in a crazy way, either. I mean in a natural, decent, kind way. Most of them are sad, of course, but not much sadder than people anywhere else." Huzinga stopped a moment. "He'll get the tiger for us all right. When that happens we'll know where we stand, at any rate, even if we won't be able to tell anybody about it. Everybody will forget the whole thing after a couple of weeks anyway. How about it?"

"No," the Chief said. "It's silly. It would get around. I'd be the laughing stock of New York."

"Today's Wednesday," Huzinga said. "We'd know in four days. Will you give *me* permission to do it? If it flops, I'll take the rap. I'll say it was my idea, I did it on my own. Pingitzer's with me. He wants to watch."

The Chief thought about all this a long time.

"O.K.," he said at last. "O.K., I'll watch, too."

"We've got to keep our promise, though," Huzinga said.

"O.K.," the Chief said. "Get going."

The Captain, glad and confident but at the same time deeply frightened, got going.

CHAPTER 13

One bright Sunday morning Tracy came up out of the earth, climbing the subway steps.

He stood in the light, looking around as he had done six years ago. The scene was not greatly changed.

He walked across Bowling Green Park to Warren Street, glanced at his watch, then hurried, as he'd always done, for the time was five minutes to eight.

Warren Street was empty. Like most Sunday streets, it seemed to be a street that was being dreamed.

Tracy saw that the place was again Otto Seyfang's. He hurried to the entrance and went in, and from the building across the street Captain Huzinga and Chief Bly saw him do so.

They had already seen Peberdy, Ringert, and Shively go in.

"Well," Chief Bly said, "I don't know how you feel, but I feel Tracy's crazier than *anybody* knows, or ever will know. How do *you* feel?"

"It's a little early," Huzinga said. "At half-past twelve, I know Laura Luthy is going to come down Warren Street, as she did six years ago."

"Well, that's nice," Chief Bly said. "Now, this work that he's going to be doing in there—it's going to *draw* the tiger away from wherever it's hiding to Otto Seyfang's, is that right?"

"Yes."

They were interrupted by the police radio, the speaker reporting all quiet.

"Now, let me go over everything again," Chief Bly said. "She'll be wearing a yellow knit dress, is that right?"

"Yes," Huzinga said.

"She'll come by around half-past twelve, is that right?"

"Yes."

"Tracy will be standing in front there, on the steps, is that right?"

"Yes."

"The girl will stop when she sees Tracy, is that right?"

"Yes."

"At that moment the tiger will appear, is that right?"

"Yes."

"Tracy will take the girl by the arm and walk down Warren Street, the tiger walking beside him, is that right?"

"Yes."

"Three doors down the block, in that empty store there that is now full of paintings of animals hanging on the walls, will be a cage, is that right?"

"Yes."

"Where'd you get the paintings?" Bly said.

"Raymond & Raymond," Huzinga said. "They're reproductions of the most famous animal paintings in the world."

"The tiger will walk into the cage, and Tracy will shut the cage, is that right?" the Chief said.

"Yes," Huzinga said.

"On the mezzanine of the store, unnoticed, are two of our younger men, Splicer and Slew, to report what they see to us later on, is that right?"

"Yes. They're there now."

"Call them."

Huzinga called, and Slew came to the 'phone. Huzinga and Slew spoke a moment.

"They're all set," Huzinga said.

"What was it you told him not to do?" the Chief said.

"He asked if he could take some photographs," Huzinga said. "He doesn't know what he's going to be observing, but he's got his camera."

"Don't you think it might be a good idea to *have* him take some pictures?" the Chief said.

"We promised we wouldn't," Huzinga said.

"This is the Police Department," the Chief said. "What do we care what we promised?"

"Even so, I don't think we'd better take any pictures," Huzinga said.

"O.K.," the Chief said. "If we've not all of us gone mad, and he *does* get the tiger in the cage, he's going to leave the store and go on down Warren Street with the girl, is that right?"

"Yes."

"Where's he going?" Bly said.

"None of our business," Huzinga said. "For a walk, I suppose."

"We're to go to the store the minute he leaves, for the reports of Splicer and Slew, is that right?"

"Yes."

"In back of the store is a moving van," the Chief said. "The tiger in the cage will be placed in the van. As soon as possible the tiger will be examined, given any care it may need, and then turned loose where it can harm no one, is that right?"

"Yes."

"Where would that be?" Bly said.

"The animal's trainer has stated that the animal was born in captivity," Huzinga said. "The place was Madison Square Garden. Tracy has asked that the tiger be turned loose in the mountains nearest New York."

"Who says it will be safe there?" the Chief said.

"The nearest mountains that are *wild*," Huzinga said. "Where people do not live."

"I'm not thinking of people," Bly said. "I'm thinking of the tiger. How's it going to live? It's liable to run into a hunter, and be shot."

"Those are *decent* chances," Huzinga said.

"That's if everything goes the way Tracy and you like to believe they're going to go," the Chief said. "What do we do if the tiger *doesn't* appear?"

The younger man looked at the older one.

"You'll *have* to fire me," Huzinga said, "so I'll resign."

"No one else knows, is that right?" Bly said.

"Just you and I," Huzinga said, "but if it flops, I resign."

"What about Tracy and the girl—if it flops?"

"I've given Dr. Scatter my word to take them both back to Bellevue," Huzinga said.

"Does Dr. Scatter know about all this?"

"No, I cooked up another story," Huzinga said. "Pingitzer knows. I mean, he knows Laura Luthy's going to meet Tracy at half-past twelve in front of Otto Seyfang's. He doesn't know anything else, though."

"Where's *he*?" Bly said.

"Tracy asked Dr. Pingitzer to sit in the Tasting Department," Huzinga said. "I saw him go in a few minutes before you arrived."

"What's he doing in there?" Bly said.

"Tracy wanted him in there."

"Does Tracy know that if the thing flops he and the girl go back to Bellevue?"

"No," Huzinga said. "That's the thing that bothers me. I *did* keep that from him. I thought I'd better. I don't feel easy about it, though."

The radio reported again at half-past eight. Again it was all quiet. The Chief telephoned his secretary.

"We've had two all quiets," he said. "I want to know exactly what's happened, *whatever* it is. Call me back."

The secretary called back and said, "All precincts report no events of any kind."

"Are you sure?"

"Yes, sir."

"Has this ever happened before?" the Chief said. "A whole New York hour with no events at all?"

"Not as far as I know," the secretary said.

"Well," Bly said to Huzinga, "*something's* happened. No episodes of any kind, not even drunks, not even a family fight, not even a petty theft, not even a disturbance of the peace in a whole New York hour."

CHAPTER 14

Back at his old job, Tracy lifted a coffee sack to his shoulder, carried it fifty yards, and set it down, but it was not easy to do.

Tracy walked with another sack from the far end of the storage room to the wall of the Tasting Department, and then another. Each time he set a sack down he wanted to go in and taste some coffee with Peberty, Ringert, Shively, and Pingitzer because he could hear them talking, although he could not make out what they were saying. But he knew it would not do to go in until he had achieved again the knack of doing the work easily, until he had begun to enjoy doing it.

He was tired after each trip. The weight of each sack on his shoulder was enormous. Several times his knees almost gave way. He couldn't understand. It was only six years ago that the work had been so easy for him. His breathing was difficult and his heart pounded each time he lifted a sack and walked with it.

He stopped at the rear window at last, to rest, to think about the problem, to look down at the alley and the things there.

Well, it was still the same: asphalt, old brick and stone, discolored wood, garbage cans, miscellaneous junk and rubbish strewn about, a stubborn old tree, a few weeds, a low arch in the brick of the building across the alley, a number of bricks having fallen loose, two of them still lying in the alley.

He needed to rest a long time, staring down at the miserable scene. It was all new once, hopeful, bright and clean, but now it was pathetic.

And yet on the next trip he longed to see it again, as a lover longs to see his beloved, lying sick in bed.

When he came back from the fifth trip and looked at the scene, he began to see beauty in it, and the next sack he lifted was the first not to make him groan.

He walked with it easier, too, and when he set it down he heard Pingitzer and the others laugh.

The next time he looked at the scene the tree was beautiful. He smiled, thinking of the years it had been there—certainly more than six, for he had seen it then, too. Its leaves weren't green, but only because the city had covered them with its dirt. It wasn't big because there wasn't earth enough for its roots to spread out in, or space enough for its branches. But what there *was* of it was there, and it *was* a tree. In all probability its patience had been rewarded from time to time by the arrival of a bird, to greet it and go, or even to stay, to build a nest in it. The tree *was* there, there was no question about that. It had been there for a long time, and was still there. Its trunk was hard and tough, bruised here and there, but for all that still strong.

Each sack Tracy lifted and carried to the wall of the Tasting Department was easier to lift and carry. The lifting and carrying of the ninth sack wasn't work at all.

It was almost nine o'clock then, there was still a great deal to be done before twelve, but Tracy stepped into the Tasting Department.

The men sat around the round table, each of them with a silver coffee-pot beside him, Pingitzer's pot percolating.

"Ah ha," Pingitzer said. "Just in time. Here is coffee, my own idea, from Vienna, long ago." He poured a cup for Tracy, lifted it, Tracy took the cup, then tasted the coffee in it. He took his time tasting it, then tasted it again.

"Good," he said.

"My own idea," Pingitzer said. "Vienna."

Tracy walked around the room, listening to the others, as he had done six years ago. When his cup was empty, he took it to Shively, who filled it for him out of *his* pot. Shively's coffee was good, too.

"Well, I've got to get back to work," Tracy said. "I've got a lot to do."

"Ah ha," Pingitzer said. "This is way of youth. This is illusion of youth. This is *fine* illusion. Was time in Vienna when Pingitzer have this way and this illusion. This was fine time, fine way, fine illusion. Ah ha. Here is Pingitzer, seventy-two, wishing no more to work, to have fine illusion."

"I'll be back after a while," Tracy said.

He went straight to the window to have another look at the alley. There was much for him to think about that he wanted to get to as slowly as possible, but at the same time get to in the next hour or two. Time had always fascinated him. He knew he didn't understand it, but he also knew that anything you ever got—anything that ever mattered—any thought—any truth—you got *instantly*. You could wait forever if you wanted to, and let it go at that, or you could get moving—moving *into* time and *with* time—working at the thought to be received, and then suddenly, from having moved into time and with time, and from having worked at the thought, get it, get it whole, get it clean, get it instantly.

But you had to stay slow somewhere inside of yourself, too, to give the arrival a place to stop. You had to be going swiftly and you had to be almost not moving at all at the same time.

There was much for Tracy to think about, much to do, and the doing of what needed to be done had to begin with Tracy working. All that needed to be done—and it was a great deal—had to begin with the doing of a simple work, had to do with the lifting and carrying of the coffee sacks.

Tracy stood a moment, smiling at the miserable scene that was also beautiful, at the enormity of the work to be done, remembering each of the matters involved but trying not to hurry them, his eyes wandering to the low arch in the old building across the alley.

He carried a half-dozen more sacks before he stopped to glance at the scene again, and this time he only *glanced*, for the work had become exhilarating and he wanted to get on with it. But during the glance it seemed to him that he had seen something. He was carrying another sack when he wondered what it had been that he'd seen, or if he'd imagined it, from having been at a time so intense with possibilities.

He decided to carry at least a half-dozen more sacks before stopping a moment again. This time he would go to the back door, open it, and go out on the steps and look from there.

When he was on the steps, not looking anywhere in particular, he thought he saw it again, and there was a deep gladness in him. It was there, whatever it was. It was there somewhere. There was no doubt about that.

He went back to work, carried three more sacks, then stepped into the Tasting Department to spend another moment with the coffee tasters.

"How does it feel after six years?" Ringert said.

"It's beginning to feel all right again," Tracy said. "How about you, Ringert?"

"Oh," Ringert said. "Can't kick, Tracy."

"Ah ha," Pingitzer said. "This kick. This is two? One. To move foot? Two. To make complaint? Can't move with foot? Can't make complaint?"

"I don't know," Ringert said. "I can move with foot all right, but not the way I *could*. And I can complain, too, but not the way I could. I used to be able to complain about anything, and it was a lot of fun. Now, I have only one thing to complain about, and I don't even want to complain about *that*."

"Is what, this thing?" Pingitzer said.

"Ringert's end."

"Ah ha. What is taste of Ringert's coffee?"

"Good," Tracy said.

"Please," Pingitzer said, holding his cup across the table to Ringert, who poured it full. Dr. Pingitzer tasted the coffee, then said, "Ah ha. Good."

Tracy carried three more sacks, then stood at the window, with his back turned to the scene, listening. He stood a long time, perhaps three minutes. There was silence in the alley. When he was not sure he had heard something, he decided he was not sure, and went back to work. Each time he came for a new sack he paused for a moment to listen again. When he'd carried six more sacks and had listened six more times, he sat on a sack, not to rest, but to be thankful, to be near things, near the inside of things, and to smile at anything that might be near.

When he was finally sure he had heard the word, he was not surprised. He did not leap to his feet. He did not turn. He said the word back very softly. After a moment he heard it again, and then very slowly he got up and lifted a sack to his shoulder and walked with it.

When he put the sack down and turned he saw the tiger.

Its appearance was pitiful, even from so far away. It was starved, sick, weak, and wounded. He went back to the pile of sacks, scarcely looking at the tiger, lifted another sack and walked off with it. On this third trip the tiger climbed to the top of the pile of sacks, spread itself flat, to rest there and watch.

Tracy and the tiger talked, but this time not with words, not even with sounds, and each of them understood.

The swift thought had arrived to stay.

When all the sacks had been moved, it was a quarter after twelve.

The coffee tasters had left the Tasting Department to go to lunch. The tiger stood beside Tracy, and then together they went down two flights of stairs to the entrance of the building. The tiger was frightened by the door to the street, and hung back. Tracy stayed near the tiger a moment, saying nothing, then went out alone, to stand on the steps, the door swinging shut behind him.

CHAPTER 15

In the second-floor room across the street Captain Huzinga and Chief Bly watched.

There, on schedule, was Thomas Tracy standing in front of Otto Seyfang's.

"What time is it?" Bly said.

"Half-past twelve," Huzinga said. "Don't you think it'll happen?"

"Something's *already* happened," Bly said. "You heard the reports on the radio every half-hour."

"Yes."

"All quiet for four full hours."

"Yes. Do you think it'll happen?"

"I don't care if it doesn't," the Chief said. "Look at him. He's no madman."

"He's mad all right," Huzinga said suddenly. "This whole thing is. I got it wrong. I misunderstood. We've got that sign up there. *Otto Seyfang's.* Otto Seyfang's been dead three years. The place is a warehouse. It's not a coffee importing house. This is *now.* It's not six years ago. He's mad all right, but not as mad as I am to have believed any of us could do the one thing that's broken the human heart since the beginning of time. It can't be done. It can't be done, that's all. I feel sorry for him. He's crazy. He doesn't know it, but he's got to go back to Bellevue, and the girl with him. Nothing's going to happen, Chief. I'm sorry. I'll resign. I believed with all my heart he could do it. It's madness to believe *that.* Nothing's going to happen."

"What about the stuff that's *already* happened?" Bly said.

"An accident," Huzinga said. "Besides, it's happened before. I happen to have studied the old records. In December, 1882, there were seven hours in which nothing was reported. In March of 1896 there were *eleven* hours, in July of 1901 *five,* in August of 1908 *nine.* It's happened before."

"Yes," the Chief said. "Well, how do you know something else didn't happen at the same time that nobody knows about? Something else happened secretly?"

"You mean, you think something's *still* going to happen?" Huzinga said.

"I say it's *already* happened," the Chief said. "And I say don't take them back to Bellevue."

"I gave Dr. Scatter my word," Huzinga said. "In a few minutes I'll take them back and resign."

"You don't have to resign," Bly said. "We can go out on a limb, can't we? We've done it before—many times. You haven't lost your job. There's nothing at stake for you here. So the thing flops. Who cares?"

"I care," Huzinga said.

Suddenly they saw Laura Luthy walking down Warren Street.

They saw Tracy and Laura meet. They saw them smile. They saw their lips move in speech. They saw Laura go up the three steps to

Tracy. They saw him put his arms around her. They saw her arms tighten around him. They saw Peberdy, Ringert, Shively, and Pingitzer standing together, watching. They saw Tracy take Laura by the arm to go, but just before going they saw Tracy reach over to the door, and open it.

He didn't open it very much, just enough.

Then they saw Tracy's tiger come out and stand beside Laura Luthy.

It was a black panther that limped on its right front foot. Except for the limp, it was the handsomest black panther anybody ever saw.

They saw Tracy and Laura Luthy and Tracy's tiger walk together down Warren Street. They saw them go into the store with the pictures of the animals hanging on the walls of it.

After a while they saw Tracy and Laura come out and walk away, toward the docks at the end of Warren Street.

And they saw that there was no longer a tiger with them.

Bly and Huzinga ran downstairs, out of the building to the street, across the street, and into the store. They found Splicer and Slew standing together, waiting for them.

"Which one of you is Slew?" Bly said.

"I am, sir," one of the men said.

"All right," Bly said. "Tell me *exactly* what you just saw."

"I saw a young man and a young woman come in here and look at every picture hanging on the walls of this store," Slew said. "I saw them go out."

"Anything else?" Bly said.

"No, sir."

"You, Splicer," Bly said. "Tell me exactly what *you* saw."

"I saw the same, sir," Splicer said.

"Are you sure?"

"Yes, sir."

"Return to your stations, please," Bly said.

The two young officers left the store.

"Well?" Bly said to Huzinga. "How about it?"

"I don't know," Huzinga said.

"You *did* see the tiger, didn't you?"

"I saw the tiger," Bly said.

"You're not just saying that, are you?" Huzinga said. "You *did* see him open the door? You did *see* the tiger come out and stand beside her, didn't you?"

"Yes, I saw it all," Bly said.

"Splicer and Slew *didn't* see the tiger," Huzinga said.

"No, they didn't," Bly said.

"And the tiger's gone," Huzinga said.

"Yes, it is," Bly said.

"What happened to the tiger?" Huzinga said.

"I don't know," the Chief said.

"Well," Huzinga said. "I'd like the rest of the day off, if it's all right with you,"

"Your work's done," Bly said. "What are you going to do? Go to a ball game?"

"No," Huzinga said. "I think I'd like to go up to St. Patrick's for a while. Then I think I'd like to go home. I can't wait to see my wife and kids again."

"Yes," the Chief said. "Well, get going."

Huzinga went from one painting in the room to the other, and then left the store and went to Saint Patrick's. Bly now looked at each of the pictures. He went back for one last look at the picture of the Arab asleep in the desert, with the lion standing over him.

Then he too left the store and went to Saint Patrick's.

That is the story of Thomas Tracy, Laura Luthy, and the tiger, which is love.

Radio Play

COLUMBIA WORKSHOP FESTIVAL
THURSDAY, AUGUST 10, 1939, 10–10:30 P.M.

CUE: Columbia Broadcasting System
.... 30 seconds ....
(EFFECT: *General noise: musical instruments and talk*)

ANNOUNCER
> (*A young man, speaking casually in the far-Western style—not like a professional radio announcer*)

Quiet, everybody. This is where the play begins.
(*The noise quiets down*)
Let's see now. Exactly—ten o'clock, Eastern Daylight Saving Time.
> (*Time gong or chime*)

What we want during the next thirty minutes is a play.

HARRY
Oh, boy.

ANNOUNCER
Quiet, Harry.
> (*Continuing*)

The play is going to be a radio play. We don't mean anything but radio. Not a movie, over the radio. Not a stage play, over the radio. We mean a radio play, over the radio.
> (*Enthusiastic, cheering music*)

As the saying is, The curtain rises. It rises on ten o'clock in New York, six o'clock in San Francisco.

HARRY
All right. Let's get going.

ANNOUNCER

Take it easy, Harry. The play is going to be easy-going in case somebody in Oklahoma listening in has got a weak heart and might get excited if we were to shout a good deal. Or in case a little boy in Wyoming or a little girl in Tennessee is listening in and might not sleep all night, troubling over some absurd fear planted in his imagination about invasion, storm, crime, or famine.

HARRY

What do you mean?

ANNOUNCER

What I mean is, we're not going to scare the children, or anybody else.

HARRY

Oh.

ANNOUNCER

Another thing we're not going to do is, we're not going to go to work and have a wonderful romance go haywire, break a million hearts.

HARRY

Why not?

ANNOUNCER

Our platform is: If you can't make people laugh, don't make them cry. Therefore, during the next half hour we won't scare people, worry them, or break their hearts.

HARRY

Come on, let's get going.

ANNOUNCER

O.K., I'll be the announcer. I haven't studied radio announcing. I didn't go to Harvard. I'm not a Yale man. And the halls of Princeton haven't echoed to the fall of my foot. I mean, you don't have to be educated to be able to talk. I'll announce. I'll just go to work and do it. O.K. One, two, three.

(Clears throat)

Ladies and gentlemen: We're all feeling fine and don't hate anybody, so we're going to start out with a little song. None of us can sing, but we think it would be pleasant if we did our best. There are two thousand million people in the world, and not more than two or three dozen of them can really sing, so why should we feel embarrassed? Or why should you, for that matter? If you feel like singing with us, O.K.

(MUSIC: *Any song, preferably something new. A mixed group of voices sing, especially the* ANNOUNCER)

(After the song)
You see? I told you we couldn't sing. But don't forget all the other people in the world who can't sing either. We've all got a right to try. Doesn't hurt anybody.
        (Hums or sings a little)
I do a lot of singing that way, but I don't suppose I'd last a month in the Metropolitan Opera. I just get a kick out of singing. I don't sing for the money. I'm like the birds when it comes to singing. I just bust loose and warble, the same as a canary. Why should they sing all the time? They live in cages, don't they? Look where we live.

HARRY
Talk, talk, talk. That's all you hear around here, it seems like.

ANNOUNCER
O.K. Here we go. Act one. A Fable. The Federal Bureau of Investigation doesn't know it yet, but I stole a watermelon once. I ate it, too. I felt bad about that for a week. It wasn't ripe, that's why. I *had* to eat it, though, because it was too big to carry in my pocket. We'll make a fable of this episode. I'll be the farmer. Harry, you be me, a small barefoot boy of ten with his stomach full of unripe watermelon. The scene is a watermelon patch in Georgia, Alabama, California, Florida, or anywhere else where watermelon grow.

HARRY
All right, Al, I'll be you, and you be the farmer.

ANNOUNCER
        (Like a farmer)
Howdy, boy. How would you like a nice ripe watermelon? The market's bad and I hate to see all the watermelon go to waste, rotting on the vines, barefoot boy, with cheeks of tan.

HARRY

What do *I* say?

ANNOUNCER

What kind of a barefoot boy with cheeks of tan are you anyway?
Say what you think you ought to say. Let's see if we can carry on
a little conversation.

HARRY

O.K.

(Like a barefoot boy with checks of tan)

Mr. Jenkins, I already ate one of your watermelons.

ANNOUNCER

Well, son, I'm delighted. You're welcome to any watermelon of
mine any time you feel in the mood.

HARRY

Yeah, but it wasn't ripe and I think I've got a stomach-ache.

ANNOUNCER

Stomach-ache? That's awful. Don't you know how to pick out a
ripe watermelon?

HARRY

I didn't have time enough.

ANNOUNCER

Didn't have time enough? Why not? It's early in the day.

HARRY

Mr. Jenkins, I was scared.

ANNOUNCER

Scared of what?

HARRY

You.

ANNOUNCER

Me? What in the world were you scared of me for?

HARRY

I was *stealing.* I was stealing one of your watermelons, Mr. Jenkins.

ANNOUNCER

My boy, you just *think* you were stealing.

HARRY

I *was* stealing, Mr. Jenkins. I came up the road, as if I was on my
way to Grandma's. All of a sudden I jumped over the fence, ran

to the watermelon patch, stole the first one I came to, and ran
back here and ate it. Now, I think I've got a stomach-ache.
> *(Like himself)*

How's that, all right?

ANNOUNCER

That was fine Harry. That was a very nice little parable we made
up—and I think it isn't going to do anybody in the world any
harm. That parable has a very pleasant moral, most likely.

HARRY

O.K. Where are we now?

ANNOUNCER

Along about this time I think we'd better hear a little music.
Something new, just composed, never before heard by anybody.
Hermann, you're a composer. Let's talk a little about that.

HERMANN

You want to talk to *me*?

ANNOUNCER

Sure. There's drama in how a young fellow like you goes to work
and composes a song, or a piece of music, or something like that.
How do you do it?

HERMANN

Well, let me see: How do I do it. I don't know *how* I do it. I mean—

ANNOUNCER

That's fine. That's all I wanted to know. Let's hear it without any
further fuss. It's probably very good.
> *(The song)*

Say, that *was* good. What's the name of that song?

HERMANN

I Like You and You Like Me and We Like Everybody. It's a love song.
I'll tell you how the idea happened to come to me. I was sitting
in the subway reading the funny paper when the fellow who was
holding the paper turned the page. All of a sudden I began to think
about how well everybody gets along with everybody else most
of the time, and then I said to myself, Hermann, I think there's a
song in that idea somewhere or other, and sure enough—

ANNOUNCER

Yes, sir, sure enough.

HERMANN
Well, you see so many songs have been written about different places and things, I always wanted to write a song about a thing that was *far away* from a place.

ANNOUNCER
That's nice. What was that title again?

HERMANN
It's kind of romantic. I call it *In a Subway Far from Ireland.*

ANNOUNCER
Thank you very much, Hermann. Now comes the Department of Education, or No Information, Thank You.
  (Cash register rings)
The idea is for me to ask six or seven of the most intelligent people here—

HARRY
Intelligent? Who?
  (Cash register rings again)

ANNOUNCER
All right, Sam, stay away from that cash register.—Intelligent people a few simple questions. You answer them. If you answer the question correctly, you win.

HARRY
Oh, boy! What's the first question?

ANNOUNCER
Just a minute, Harry. Ladies and gentlemen. Six of the most intelligent personalities on this floor of the Columbia Broadcasting System Building in New York have been brought here, at tremendous expense and with the help of ropes, chains, pulleys, levers and trap-doors, for the purpose of answering miscellaneous questions sent in by a school girl in Altoona, Pennsylvania. These six experts are all named Harry, and are regarded as above average.

HARRY
Above average in what?

ANNOUNCER
Height, weight, and size of hat. What size hat do you wear, Harry?

HARRY
Ah, what's the question?

(Cash register rings)

ANNOUNCER

Now, Sam, I told you to get away from that cash register. What do you think you're doing?

SAM

I'm trying to get my hand out of it. How does this thing work?

ANNOUNCER

What'd you do, get your hand caught in the cash register?

SAM

Yeah.

ANNOUNCER

What'd you put your hand in there for in the first place?

SAM

I never saw a cash register come out and go back in so quickly. I just wanted to *touch* the money.

ANNOUNCER

Here. Let me get you out of this. You been to high school?

SAM

Yeah, but get my hand out of this, will you?

ANNOUNCER

All right. I'll ring No Sale. You draw your hand out real quick. It works faster than the eye, you know. Ready?

SAM

O.K.

ANNOUNCER

I'll count to three. One. Two. Three.
    (Cash register rings. Swift sound of drawer moving out and back in)
There you are, Sam.

SAM

Yeah, now my tie's caught.

ANNOUNCER

All right, again. One. Two. Three.
    (Same business)
O.K. now?

SAM

O.K. Thanks. Gosh! Was I scared?

ANNOUNCER
You can't fool with these modern conveniences.

HARRY
What's the question? I got a whole education going to waste over here.

ANNOUNCER
What is it that is white all around, has four windows and never moves?

HARRY
Is that the question?

ANNOUNCER
It isn't the answer.

HARRY
Read it again.

ANNOUNCER
Now, listen carefully. What is it that has a porch, four numbers by the door, and doesn't talk?

HARRY
Was that the question you read the first time?

ANNOUNCER
Answer the question, will you? There's a time limit, you know. Five minutes. Precious time is going by. Hurry.

HARRY
Let's see now—no wheels, smoke doesn't come out, and never worries. W. Shakespeare?

ANNOUNCER
No.

HARRY
Am I warm?

ANNOUNCER
Answer the question.

HARRY
Gilbert and Sullivan?

ANNOUNCER
(Irritated)
No. You're guessing.

HARRY

  Well, what is it then?

ANNOUNCER

  I'm *asking* the questions? You're answering them.

HARRY

  Well, I give up. What is it?

ANNOUNCER

  Let's see.

      (*Shuffling papers*)

  It doesn't say.

HARRY

  What was the question again?

ANNOUNCER

  All right, once more, but that's all. Listen carefully. What is it
  that stays in one place all the time and never does anything
  unless it catches on fire or is torn down, and where if you live
  there and write letters to people letters come to you?

HARRY

  Clifton Fadiman!

ANNOUNCER

  Ah, you're thinking of something else.

HARRY

  No, I'm not. Isn't it Clifton?

ANNOUNCER

  I don't think so. I'm not sure, though.

HARRY

  Sure, it is. Clifton Fadiman. That's the answer.

ANNOUNCER

  Well, all right, but it doesn't seem *exactly* right.

HARRY

  Sure, it is.

ANNOUNCER

  O.K. Ring the cash register, Sam.

      (*Cash register rings*)

  Did you get the money for Harry?

SAM

  I'd like to see anybody get anything out of this cash register.

ANNOUNCER

>Let's all work together. I'll ring No Sale and when the drawer comes out, you and Harry grab it and hold it open and I'll get the money.

SAM

>I'll do my best.
>
>>*(Cash register rings, drawer comes out, moves right back in)*

ANNOUNCER

>Ooooop. Missed it that time. Try it again.
>
>>*(Rings it again)*
>
>Try harder, will you?

HARRY

>Come on, now. Don't try to gyp me. Give me my money.

ANNOUNCER

>Take it easy, Harry. You answered the question and you're going to get your money. First we've got to hold the drawer out.

HARRY

>No finagling, please.

ANNOUNCER

>O.K. Once more, but this time more speed and more efficiency. Let's have a little accuracy around here.
>
>*(Cash register rings, same business)*

SAM

>Ah, heck. This thing's too fast.

ANNOUNCER

>Here. You ring No Sale, Sam. I'll hold it open.

SAM

>Look out for your fingers. That's all I've got to say.
>
>>*(Cash register rings—drawer comes out—announcer grabs— the sound of the business gets labored)*

ANNOUNCER

>I've got it.
>
>>*(The drawer snaps back)*
>
>Ouuuuuuuuuhhhhhh! Get my hand out of here.

SAM

>You see?
>
>>*(Cash register rings again)*

ANNOUNCER

Oh, boy. Say, Harry, I'll have to owe you the money.

HARRY

Nothing doing. Pay me—now.

ANNOUNCER

Now, don't be technical.

HARRY

I answered the question. And I want my money. A bargain is a bargain.

ANNOUNCER

All right. Get your money out of the cash register yourself.

HARRY

All right, I will. Can't scare *me*.

> (*Cash register rings, drawer comes out—same slowing down of business and it snaps back into place*)

Ouuuuuuh!

ANNOUNCER

O.K., Sam. Get his hand out of there.

> (*Cash register rings*)

Now, are you satisfied?

HARRY

I want my money.

ANNOUNCER

Second question.

HARRY

I won't talk.

ANNOUNCER

Ah, come on now, Harry. What is it that has bad manners and is very fat?

HARRY

Can it move?

ANNOUNCER

Yeah, sure, if it isn't dead.

HARRY

A tiger.

ANNOUNCER

Tigers aren't fat.

HARRY

They've got bad manners.

ANNOUNCER

Not necessarily. That isn't the answer.

HARRY

Tigers sometimes get fat, and don't ever forget it.

ANNOUNCER

As a rule, tigers aren't fat. We've got to go by the average.

HARRY

Let me think. Bad manners and fat. There's a guy over in Jersey—

ANNOUNCER

No, no.

HARRY

What's the question again?

 (Cash register rings)

SAM

Ouuuuuuh!

ANNOUNCER

Serves you right.

SAM

I'm getting burned up around here. All I want to do is *look* at the money.

ANNOUNCER

Get your hand out of there and stay away from that machine. It's treacherous.

 (Cash register rings again)

HARRY

What's the question?

ANNOUNCER

Who was it made a mistake and came to America in 1492?

HARRY

Bad manners and fat. Are you sure it was 1492?

ANNOUNCER

That's what it says here.

HARRY

Who is this girl in Altoona, Pennsylvania, anyway?

 (The cash register rings)

SAM

Ouuuuuh!

ANNOUNCER

The scene changes along about here, I believe, and everybody gets serious, especially me.

> *(Very seriously, like all radio speakers who mean to put over something subtly, with the help of a sledge-hammer)*

There is an old saying that a stitch in time saves nine, but a message of this sort, we may very well suppose, can be taken with a grain of salt. We are not saying that the present administration should discontinue spending. We are saying that a bird in the hand is worth two in the bush. We have no sympathy for people who will not understand that there are good reasons for *some* of the spending. What we say is, *Who* is going to *pay* the debt? Shall *I* pay it? Shall *you*? If so, what are we going to pay it *with,* if we have no money? And when all our money is gone, where shall we get new money from? If we spend, are we sure there will be a greater and nobler national art, a finer American culture? Can we hope for any solution to everything if the money goes, and goes, and goes, and keeps going, and—

HARRY

Say, Al, what do you think you're doing?

ANNOUNCER

Thanks, Harry. I got a little carried away there, I guess. What I mean is, don't you see, and so forth and so on.

HARRY

Al, this is supposed to be a play even *children* can understand. How can *anybody* understand that kind of talk?

ANNOUNCER

Why should anybody understand *me* talking that way when they haven't understood anybody else talking that way over the radio in the last ten years? I just want everybody to know what that kind of talk amounts to. Nothing, that's what. I want the children to know.

HARRY

Well, let's imagine they've found out, and go on to the opera part of the play.

ANNOUNCER
Are we going to have some opera? That's swell. I can sing again.

HARRY
We're going to have some opera, but *without singing.*

ANNOUNCER
How can you have opera without singing?

HARRY
This is special opera. We're just going to *hear the music.*

ANNOUNCER
You've *got* to have singing in an opera.

HARRY
O.K., then. A few of us will shout.

ANNOUNCER
Oh, boy. Wait till you hear me. But let's do that opera a little later. Let's *sell* something first.

HARRY
We haven't got anything to sell.

ANNOUNCER
Let's sell something anyway. Who wants to sell something? Hank, get in here and sell something.

HANK
Who, me?

ANNOUNCER
Yeah, *go* ahead.

HANK
O.K. Ladies and gentlemen, if you've got some extra money and feel like buying something or other, go ahead and buy it and we hope you enjoy it. Buy anything. Buy anything you feel like buying. You know how much money you've got, and how much you can spare, and what you need most, and what you like most, so we don't need to tell you what to get. Almost everything they're selling is very good, and if we had a little extra money ourselves, we'd go right out and buy us a little something or other.

HARRY
This doesn't sound like a play. It hasn't got a plot.

ANNOUNCER
No *plot?* Why, Harry, this is *all* plot. We've got a great little drama here.

HARRY
Yeah, but she doesn't tell him she loves him.

ANNOUNCER
We can take care of that. Here.
    (Calling)
Alice.

ALICE
What do you want?

ANNOUNCER
Alice, do you suppose you could tell Johnny over there you love him, so we could get a little love interest in here somewhere?

ALICE
Johnny?

ANNOUNCER
That's fine. All right, Johnny, come on over here and listen to Alice telling you.

JOHNNY
Yeah, but I really *am* in love with Alice.

ANNOUNCER
Well, so much the better. Here's your chance to convey the message to her.

JOHNNY
Convey it? I've been conveying it to her three months now. Do you think she cares?

ANNOUNCER
Alice, don't you?

ALICE
I'm kind of in love with somebody else.

JOHNNY
You see?

ANNOUNCER
Now, now, Alice, don't be finicky. Johnny's a nice boy.

ALICE
He isn't romantic.

JOHNNY
I am *too* romantic. I've seen all the movies, and I guess I know how to behave in a romance.

ALICE

Well, you're not romantic *enough*.

JOHNNY

Oh, yeah? Well, who was it pointed out the moon to you the other night?

ALICE

That moon! No bigger than a slice of watermelon.

JOHNNY

What do you want me to do, control the seasons? It was the only moon there was at the time, and I pointed it out to you. Remember?

(*Romantically*)

Remember how I held your hand and said, Look, Alice, the moon!

ALICE

Yeah, I remember. Remember how I said, Let's go to a show or a night club or a movie or something, and you said, How much money you got?

JOHNNY

Well, I was broke. All I had was twenty-seven cents. It wasn't my fault. The trouble with you, Alice, is—

ANNOUNCER

All right, all right, now. Alice, you go ahead now and tell Johnny you love him.

ALICE

O.K., but it's going to be an exaggeration.

ANNOUNCER

Now, Alice. People are listening.

ALICE

O.K. Johnny, I love you.

ANNOUNCER

Oh, that'll never do. You know very well you can do better than that. Now, try again.

ALICE

Johnny, I love you.

JOHNNY

It doesn't have the ring of truth. It sounds like a hollow mockery to me.

ANNOUNCER

Just a minute, Johnny. I'll get this romance on its feet. Now, once again, Alice.

ALICE

This is maximum.
        (Very romantically)
Johnny, I love you.

JOHNNY
        (Amazed)
Alice!

ANNOUNCER
        (Whispering)
Tell him some more, Alice.

ALICE

Johnny, I love you.

JOHNNY

I love you, too, Alice.

ALICE
        (Loudly)
You see? He takes advantage of the situation.

ANNOUNCER

That was fine. That was just right to give everybody an idea. That's all we wanted to do. Just give them an idea.

ALICE

You see, Al, Johnny—

ANNOUNCER

That's all, Alice. You can go back to the orchestra-leader now.

ALICE

I mean, he hasn't got—

ANNOUNCER

All we wanted to do was—

JOHNNY

She's selfish and—

ANNOUNCER

That's all, Johnny. All we wanted to do was give them an idea. Now you go back to—

ALICE

Who's selfish?

JOHNNY

Alice, you know I love you, but you know you are selfish.

ANNOUNCER

Will you two please argue this out somewhere else? All I wanted to do was give the people an idea. Now let's do something super.

HARRY

Super? What do you mean, super?

ANNOUNCER

(*Hedging*)

Well, all right then, *ordinary.* Can't a fellow have a little fun once in a while? This isn't going to be super *exactly,* but what's the harm in saying it is? Everybody else does.

HARRY

Well, what *is* it going to be? *Exactly?*

ANNOUNCER

Give me a little time. All I know is, it's got to have a drum roll with it. Roll the drum over there, will you, George?

(*Drum roll*)

HARRY

All right, the drum's rolling, so what?

ANNOUNCER

Wait a minute. Give me time. Why don't you co-operate a little? What's good after a drum roll?

HARRY

War?

ANNOUNCER

No, that's dated. What else?

HARRY

Well, somebody could stick his head in a lion's mouth, or something like that.

ANNOUNCER

No, let's do something dangerous.

HARRY

For instance?

ANNOUNCER

How about a wedding?

HARRY

That's been done.

ANNOUNCER

How about a divorce?

DRUMMER

Hey, how long do I have to do this? My arms are getting tired.

ANNOUNCER

Well, you can stop for a minute, George, but bang around. We'll get this thing figured out if it takes all week.

DRUMMER

When do we go on the air?

ANNOUNCER

When? We're on the air now.

DRUMMER

Holy Moses! I can't say lines.

ANNOUNCER

Now don't get self-conscious, you're doing fine.

DRUMMER

Fine? Anybody would think I was an actor. Nobody would know I stutter.

HARRY

All right, Al, what's it going to be?

ANNOUNCER

It's got to be dangerous, dramatic, educational, portable, entertaining, and—

HARRY

Dangerous? How about a murder?

ANNOUNCER

You mean, just in fun?

HARRY

Sure. What do you think I mean? We wouldn't want to have somebody permanently murdered, would we?

ANNOUNCER

No, I guess not. Let's have somebody murdered that nobody in the world likes. He's a guy that goes around making trouble everywhere, hurting people's feelings, and never lending anybody a nickel. George, roll the drums again. We're all set.

(The drum rolls. Heavy, melodramatic footsteps coming)
(Whispering)

Here he is now. Hand me that machine-gun, Harry.

HARRY
    O.K., Al.
ANNOUNCER
    He's coming closer now.
HARRY
    Don't you think we ought to give him another chance, Al?
ANNOUNCER
    Well, all right—ask him to lend you a nickel.
HARRY
        (Awkwardly)
    Excuse me, could you spare a nickel for a cup of coffee?
VILLAIN
    No.
HARRY
    Ah, come on, be a sport. I'm nervous and I need a cup of coffee.
VILLAIN
    Nothing doing.
HARRY
    What's a nickel?
VILLAIN
    Plenty.
HARRY
    If I don't have a cup of coffee soon, I'll probably die.
VILLAIN
    Go ahead and die.
HARRY
        (Burned up)
    All right, Al, let him have it. He's no good.
        (The drum roll gets real dramatic)
ANNOUNCER
    O.K. Here goes.
        (The drum stops rolling. ANNOUNCER *fires a pop-gun)*
VILLAIN
        (High-pitched wail)
    Oooouuch!
ANNOUNCER
    Serves you right.

VILLAIN

I didn't do anything. It ain't fair.

ANNOUNCER

You be kind to others, and others will be kind to you. Otherwise, bang!

>   *(He pops the gun again)*

VILLAIN

Oouuch! I'm getting out of here.

ANNOUNCER

Let that be a lesson to you.

HARRY

>   *(Excited)*

Hey, Al, we've only got five minutes to go.

ANNOUNCER

So what? Five minutes is a long time and we've got nothing to do.

HARRY

Yeah, but what'll people think?

ANNOUNCER

What do you mean?

HARRY

I mean, all we've got is five minutes to go, and so far nothing's happened.

ANNOUNCER

Does something have to happen?

HARRY

Something usually does in a play.

ANNOUNCER

Yeah, but *what kind* of a play? Some little unimportant saga of some kind.

HARRY

People won't like a play like this, where nothing happens.

ANNOUNCER

Don't worry about people. Now let's go ahead with the opera.

HARRY

Oh, boy.

>   (MUSIC: *Opera music, during which everybody around, especially the* ANNOUNCER, *shouts. There is a very dramatic wind-up)*

Now, that's what I call opera. Let's do it again. What do you say, Al?

ANNOUNCER

Wait a minute, boys. We haven't got time. Only a minute and a half left. Tell you what let's do. We'll dedicate a minute of silence—a whole minute of dead air—to music lovers everywhere.

(*Silence begins. Cough*)

Sh-h-h.

(SOUND: *Loud telephone bell*)

Sh-h-h.

(SOUND: *Bell gets quieter…receiver up*)

Hello. Yeah. Yeah. Well, this is a fine time to call up. We're having a one-minute silence.

(*Loud*)

I said we're having a one-minute silence. I can't tell you the story of the play now. I don't know the story. I'm only the announcer.

(SOUND: *Phone up*)

All right, our minute of silence is up. Now, wasn't that peaceful?

HARRY

I still don't think they're going to like this play.

ANNOUNCER

Did you like it?

HARRY

Me? Sure. I was *in* it.

ANNOUNCER

Well, everybody else was in it, too. You can't keep people out of a radio play.

ALL

(*Noise and talk again as at the beginning of the play*)

ANNOUNCER

Quiet, everybody. The play's not quite over yet.

ALL

(*Everybody becomes quiet gradually*)

ANNOUNCER

Ladies and gentlemen, *Radio Play*, written for the Columbia Workshop by William Saroyan, is *now* over. Thank you for listening.

from *The Human Comedy*

CHAPTER 1   *Ulysses*

The little boy named Ulysses Macauley one day stood over the new
gopher hole in the backyard of his house on Santa Clara Avenue in
Ithaca, California. The gopher of this hole pushed up fresh moist
dirt and peeked out at the boy, who was certainly a stranger but perhaps not an enemy. Before this miracle had been fully enjoyed by
the boy, one of the birds of Ithaca flew into the old walnut tree in
the backyard and after settling itself on a branch broke into rap-
ture, moving the boy's fascination from the earth to the tree. Next,
best of all, a freight train puffed and roared far away. The boy listened, and felt the earth beneath him tremble with the moving of
the train. Then he broke into running, moving (it seemed to him)
swifter than any life in the world.

When he reached the crossing he was just in time to see the passing of the whole train, from locomotive to caboose. He waved to the
engineer, but the engineer did not wave back to him. He waved to
five others who were with the train, but not one of them waved
back. They might have done so, but they didn't. At last a Negro
appeared leaning over the side of a gondola. Above the clatter of the
train, Ulysses heard the man singing:

> "Weep no more, my lady. O weep no more today
> We will sing one song for the old Kentucky home
> For the old Kentucky home far away"

Ulysses waved to the Negro too, and then a wondrous and unexpected thing happened. *This* man, black and different from all the
others, waved back to Ulysses, shouting: "Going home, boy—going
back where I belong!"

The small boy and the Negro waved to one another until the train was almost out of sight.

Then Ulysses looked around. There it was, all around him, funny and lonely—the world of his life. The strange, weed-infested, junky, wonderful, senseless yet beautiful world. Walking down the track came an old man with a rolled bundle on his back. Ulysses waved to this man too, but the man was too old and too tired to be pleased with a small boy's friendliness. The old man glanced at Ulysses as if both he and the boy were already dead.

The little boy turned slowly and started for home. As he moved, he still listened to the passing of the train, the singing of the Negro, and the joyous words: "Going home, boy—going back where I belong!" He stopped to think of all this, loitering beside a china-ball tree and kicking at the yellow, smelly, fallen fruit of it. After a moment he smiled the smile of the Macauley people—the gentle, wise, secret smile which said *Yes* to all things.

When he turned the corner and saw the Macauley house, Ulysses began to skip, kicking up a heel. He tripped and fell because of this merriment, but got to his feet and went on.

His mother was in the yard, throwing feed to the chickens. She watched the boy trip and fall and get up and skip again. He came quickly and quietly and stood beside her, then went to the hen nest to look for eggs. He found one. He looked at it a moment, picked it up, brought it to his mother and very carefully handed it to her, by which he meant what no man can guess and no child can remember to tell.

CHAPTER 2   *Homer*

His brother Homer sat on the seat of a secondhand bicycle which struggled bravely with the dirt of a country road. Homer Macauley wore a telegraph messenger's coat which was far too big and a cap which was not quite big enough. The sun was going down in a somnolence of evening peace deeply cherished by the people of Ithaca. All about the messenger orchards and vineyards rested in the old, old earth of California. Even though he was moving along swiftly, Homer was not missing any of the charm of the region. Look at that! he kept saying to himself of earth and tree, sun and grass and cloud. Look at that, will you? He began to make decorations with the movements of his bike and, to accompany these ornaments of movement, he burst out with a shouting of music—simple, lyrical and ridiculous. The theme of this opera was taken over in his mind by the strings of an orchestra, then supplemented by the harp of his mother and the piano of his sister Bess. And finally, to bring the whole family together, an accordion came into the group, saying the music with a smiling and somber sweetness, as Homer remembered his brother Marcus.

Homer's music fled before the hurrying clatter of three incredible objects moving across the sky. The messenger looked up at these objects, and promptly rode into a small dry ditch. Airplanes, Homer said to himself. A farmer's dog came swiftly and with great importance, barking like a man with a message. Homer ignored the message, turning only once to spoof the animal by saying "Arp, Arp!" He seated himself on the bicycle again and rode on.

When he reached the beginning of the residential district of the city, he passed a sign without reading it:

ITHACA, CALIFORNIA
EAST, WEST—HOME IS BEST
WELCOME, STRANGER

He stopped at the next corner to behold a long line of Army trucks full of soldiers roll by. He saluted the men, just as his brother Ulysses had waved to the engineer and the hoboes. A great many soldiers returned the messenger's salute. Why not? What did they know about anything?

CHAPTER 3   *You Go Your Way, I'll Go Mine*

The messenger got off his bicycle in front of the house of Mrs. Rosa Sandoval. He went to the door and knocked gently. He knew almost immediately that someone was inside the house. He could not hear anything, but he was sure the knock was bringing someone to the door and he was most eager to see who this person would be—this woman named Rosa Sandoval who was now to hear of murder in the world and to feel it herself. The door was not a long time in opening, but there was no hurry in the way it moved on its hinges. The movement of the door was as if, whoever she was, she had nothing in the world to fear. Then the door was open, and there she was.

To Homer the Mexican woman was beautiful. He could see that she had been patient all her life, so that now, after years of it, her lips were set in a gentle and saintly smile. But like all people who never receive telegrams the appearance of a messenger at the front door is full of terrible implications. Homer knew that Mrs. Rosa Sandoval was shocked to see him. Her first word was the first word of all surprise. She said "Oh," as if instead of a messenger she had thought of opening the door to someone she had known a long time and would be pleased to sit down with. Before she spoke again she studied Homer's eyes and Homer knew that she knew the message was not a welcome one.

"You have a telegram?" she said.

It wasn't Homer's fault. His work was to deliver telegrams. Even so, it seemed to him that he was part of the whole mistake. He felt awkward and almost as if he *alone* were responsible for what had happened. At the same time he wanted to come right out and say, "I'm only a messenger, Mrs. Sandoval. I'm very sorry I must bring you a telegram like this, but it is only because it is my work to do so."

"Who is it for?" the Mexican woman said.

"Mrs. Rosa Sandoval, 1129 G Street," Homer said. He extended the telegram to the Mexican woman, but she would not touch it.

"Are you Mrs. Sandoval?" Homer said.

"Please," the woman said. "Please come in. I cannot read English. I am Mexican. I read only *La Prensa* which comes from Mexico City." She paused a moment and looked at the boy standing awkwardly as near the door as he could be and still be inside the house.

"Please," she said, "what does the telegram say?"

"Mrs. Sandoval," the messenger said, "the telegram says—"

But now the woman interrupted him. "But you must *open* the telegram and *read* it to me," she said. "You have not opened it."

"Yes, ma'am," Homer said as if he were speaking to a school teacher who had just corrected him.

He opened the telegram with nervous fingers. The Mexican woman stooped to pick up the torn envelope, and tried to smooth it out. As she did so she said, "Who sent the telegram—my son Juan Domingo?

"No, ma'am," Homer said. "The telegram is from the War Department."

"War Department?" the Mexican woman said.

"Mrs. Sandoval," Homer said swiftly, "your son is dead. Maybe it's a mistake. Everybody makes a mistake, Mrs. Sandoval. Maybe it wasn't your son. Maybe it was somebody else. The telegram *says* it was Juan Domingo. But maybe the telegram is wrong."

The Mexican woman pretended not to hear.

"Oh, do not be afraid," she said. "Come inside. Come inside. I will bring you candy." She took the boy's arm and brought him to the table at the center of the room and there she made him sit.

"All boys like candy," she said. "I will bring you candy." She went into another room and soon returned with an old chocolate candy box. She opened the box at the table and in it Homer saw a strange kind of candy.

"Here," she said. "Eat this candy. All boys like candy."

Homer took a piece of the candy from the box, put it into his mouth, and tried to chew.

"You would not bring me a bad telegram," she said. "You are a good boy—like my little Juanito when he was a little boy. Eat another piece." And she made the messenger take another piece of the candy.

Homer sat chewing the dry candy while the Mexican woman talked. "It is our own candy," she said, "from cactus. I make it for my Juanito when he come home, but *you* eat it. You are my boy too."

Now suddenly she began to sob, holding herself in as if weeping were a disgrace. Homer wanted to get up and run but he knew he would stay. He even thought he might stay the rest of his life. He just didn't know what else to do to try to make the woman less unhappy, and if she had *asked* him to take the place of her son, he would not have been able to refuse, because he would not have known how. He got to his feet as if by standing he meant to begin correcting what could not be corrected and then he knew the foolishness of this intention and became more awkward than ever. In his heart he was saying over and over again, "What can I do? What the hell can *I* do? I'm only the messenger."

The woman suddenly took him in her arms, saying, "My little boy, my little boy!"

He didn't know why, because he only felt wounded by the whole thing, but for some reason he was sickened through all his blood and thought he would need to vomit. He didn't *dislike* the woman or anybody else, but what was happening to her seemed so wrong and so full of ugliness that he was sick and didn't know if he ever wanted to go on living again.

"Come now," the woman said. "Sit down here." She forced him into another chair and stood over him. "Let me look at you," she said. She looked at him strangely and, sick everywhere within himself, the messenger could not move. He felt neither love nor hate but something very close to disgust, but at the same time he felt great compassion, not for the poor woman alone, but for all things and the ridiculous way of their enduring and dying. He saw her back in time, a beautiful young woman sitting beside the crib of her infant son. He saw her looking down at this amazing human thing, speechless and helpless and full of the world to come. He saw her rocking the crib and he heard her singing to the child. Now look at her, he said to himself.

He was on his bicycle suddenly, riding swiftly down the dark street, tears coming out of his eyes and his mouth whispering young and crazy curses. When he got back to the telegraph office the tears had stopped, but everything else had started and he knew there would be no stopping them. "Otherwise I'm just as good as dead myself," he said, as if someone were listening whose hearing was not perfect.

CHAPTER 4   *A Speech on the Human Nose*

Miss Hicks waited for Helen to take her seat and then looked over the faces of her pupils. "Now," she said, "what have we learned?"

"That people all over the world have noses," Homer said.

Miss Hicks was not upset by this reply and took it for what it was worth. "What else?" she said.

"That noses," Homer said, "are not only for blowing or to have colds in but also to keep the record of ancient history straight."

Miss Hicks turned away from Homer and said, "Someone else, please. Homer seems to have been carried away by the noses."

"Well, it's in the book, isn't it?" Homer said. "What do *they* mention it for? It must be important."

"Perhaps," Miss Hicks said, "you would like to make an extemporaneous speech on the nose, Mr. Macauley."

"Well," Horner said, "maybe not exactly a speech—but ancient history tells us one thing." Slowly now, and with a kind of unnecessary emphasis, he continued, "People have always had noses. To prove it all you have to do is look around at everybody in this classroom." He looked around at everybody. "Noses," he said, "all over the place." He stopped a moment to decide what else would be possible to say on this theme. "The nose," he decided to say, "is perhaps the most ridiculous part of the human face. It has always been a source of embarrassment to the human race, and the Hittites probably beat up on everybody because their noses were so big and crooked. It doesn't matter who invented the sundial because sooner or later somebody invents a watch. The important thing is, Who's got the noses?"

Joe the comedian listened with profound interest and admiration, if not envy. Homer continued.

"Some people," he said, "talk through their noses. A great many people snore through their noses, and a handful of people whistle or sing through them. Some people are led around by their noses, others use the nose for prying and poking into miscellaneous places. Noses have been bitten by mad dogs and movie actors in passionate love stories. Doors have been slammed on them and they have been caught in egg-beaters and automatic record changers. The nose is stationary, like a tree, but being on a movable object— the head—it suffers great punishment by being taken to places where it is only in the way. The purpose of the nose is to smell what's in the air, but some people sniff with the nose at other people's ideas, manners, or appearances." He turned and looked at Hubert Ackley III and then at Helen Eliot, whose nose, instead of moving upward, for some reason went slightly downward. "These people," he said, "generally hold their noses toward heaven, as if that were the way to get in. Most animals have nostrils but few have noses, as we understand noses, yet the sense of smell in animals is more

highly developed than in man—who has a nose, and no fooling."
Homer Macauley took a deep breath and decided to conclude his
speech. "The most important thing about the nose," he said, "is that
it makes trouble, causes wars, breaks up old friendships, and wrecks
many happy homes. *Now* can I go to the track meet, Miss Hicks?"

The ancient-history teacher, although pleased with this imagi-
native discourse on a trivial theme, would not allow its success to
interfere with the need for her to maintain order in her classroom.
"You will stay in after school, Mr. Macauley," she said, "and *you*, Mr.
Ackley. Now that we have disposed of the matter of noses, someone
else please comment on what we have read."

There were no comments.

"Come, come now," Miss Hicks said. "Somebody else comment—
anybody."

Joe the comedian answered the call. "Noses are red," he said, "vio-
lets are blue. This class is dead. And in all probability so are you."

"Anyone else?" Miss Hicks said.

"Big noses are generally on navigators and explorers," a girl said.

"All two-headed boys have two noses," Joe said.

"The nose is never on the back of the head," one of Joe's admirers
said.

"Somebody else," Miss Hicks said. She turned to a boy and said
his name. "Henry?"

"I don't know anything about noses," Henry said.

Joe turned to Henry. "All right," he said, "who is Moses?"

"Moses was in the Bible," Henry said.

"Did he have a nose?" Joe said.

"Sure he had a nose," Henry said.

"All right, then," Joe said. "Why don't you say, 'Moses had a nose
as big as most noses'? This is an ancient history class. Why don't
you try to learn something once in a while? Moses—noses—
ancient—history. Catch on?"

Henry tried to catch on. "Moses noses," he said. "No, wait a minute.
Moses's nose was a big nose."

"Ah," Joe said. "You'll never learn anything. You'll die in the
poorhouse. Moses had a nose as big as most noses! Henry, you've got
to get that straight. Now think about it."

"All right, now," Miss Hicks said, "anybody else?"

"The hand is faster than the eye," Joe said, "but only the nose runs."

"Miss Hicks," Homer said, "you've got to let me run the two-twenty low hurdles."

"I'm not interested in *any* kind of hurdles," Miss Hicks said. "Now, anyone else?"

"Well," Homer said, "I brought this class to life for you, didn't I? I've got them all talking about noses, haven't I?"

"That's beside the point," the ancient-history teacher said. "Somebody else now?"

But it was too late. The class bell rang. Everyone got up to leave for the track meet except Homer Macauley and Hubert Ackley III.[...]

CHAPTER 6   *At the Public Library*

The good friends, Lionel and Ulysses, walked toward the public library. A block before them a funeral procession emerged from the First Ithaca Presbyterian Church. Pallbearers carried a plain casket to an old Packard hearse. Following the casket the two boys saw a handful of mourners.

"Come on, Ulysses," Lionel said, "it's a funeral! Somebody's dead." They ran, Lionel holding Ulysses by the hand, and very soon they were at the center of everything.

"That's the casket," Lionel whispered. "Somebody's dead in there. I wish I knew who it is. See the flowers. They give them flowers when they die. See them crying. Those are the people who knew him."

Lionel turned to a man who wasn't very busy crying. The man had just blown his nose and touched his handkerchief to the corners of his eyes.

"Who's dead?" Lionel asked the man.

"It's poor little Johnny Merryweather, the hunchback," the man said.

Lionel turned to Ulysses. "It's poor little Johnny Merryweather, the hunchback," Lionel said.

"Seventy years old," the man said.

"Seventy years old," Lionel said to Ulysses.

"Sold popcorn on the corner of Mariposa and Broadway for thirty years," the man said.

"Sold popcorn on the corner of—" Lionel stopped suddenly and looked at the man. He almost shouted. "You mean the popcorn man?" Lionel said.

"Yes," the man said, "Johnny Merryweather—gone to his rest."

"I knew *him*!" Lionel shouted. "I bought popcorn off of him many times! Did *he* die?"

"Yes," the man said, "he died peacefully. Died in his sleep. Gone to his Maker."

"I knew Johnny Merryweather!" Lionel said, almost crying. "I didn't know his name was Johnny Merryweather, but I knew him."

Lionel turned to Ulysses and put his arm around his friend. "It's Johnny," he almost wept. "Johnny Merryweather, gone to his Maker. One of my best friends, gone to his rest."

The hearse drove away and very soon there was no one in front of the church except Lionel and Ulysses. Somehow it seemed wrong for Lionel to leave the place where he learned that the man who had died, the man in the casket, was a man he knew, even though he had never known that the man's name was Johnny Merryweather. At last, however, he decided that he couldn't stand in front of the church forever, even if he had bought popcorn off of Johnny Merryweather many times—so, thinking of the popcorn, almost tasting it again, he went on down the street with his friend Ulysses, still headed for the public library.

When the two boys entered this humble but impressive building, they entered an area of profound and almost frightening silence. It seemed as if even the walls had become speechless, and the floor and the tables, as if silence had engulfed everything in the building. There were old men reading newspapers. There were town philosophers. There were high school boys and girls doing research, but everyone was hushed, because they were seeking wisdom. They were near books. They were trying to find out. Lionel not only whispered, he moved on tiptoe. Lionel whispered because he was under the impression that it was out of respect for books, not consideration for readers. Ulysses followed him, also on tiptoe, and they explored the library, each finding many treasures, Lionel—

books, and Ulysses—people. Lionel didn't read books and he hadn't come to the public library to get any for himself. He just liked to see them—the thousands of them. He pointed out a whole row of shelved books to his friend and then he whispered, "All of these—and these. And these. Here's a red one. All these. There's a green one. All these."

Finally Mrs. Gallagher, the old librarian, noticed the two boys and went over to them. *She* didn't whisper, however. She spoke right out, as if she were not in the public library at all. This shocked Lionel and made a few people look up from the pages of their books.

"What are you looking for, boy?" Mrs. Gallagher said to Lionel.

"Books," Lionel whispered softly.

"What books are you looking for?" the librarian said.

"All of them," Lionel said.

"All of them?" the librarian said. "What do you mean? You can't borrow more than four books on one card."

"I don't want to borrow *any* of them," Lionel said.

"Well, what in the world *do* you want with them?" the librarian said.

"I just want to look at them," Lionel said.

"Look at them?" the librarian said. "That is not what the public library is for. You can look *into* them, you can look *at* the pictures in them, but what in the world do you want to look at the outsides of them for?"

"I like to," Lionel whispered. "Can't I?"

"Well," the librarian said, "there's no law against it." She looked at Ulysses. "And who's this?" she said.

"This here's Ulysses," Lionel said. "He can't read."

"Can you?" the librarian said to Lionel.

"No," Lionel said, "but he can't either. That's why we're friends. He's the only other man I know who can't read."

The old librarian looked at the two friends a moment and in her mind said something which very nearly approached a kind of delicious cursing. This was something brand new in all the years of her experience at the public library. "Well," she said at last, "perhaps it's just as well that you *can't* read. I can read. I have been reading books for the past sixty years, and I can't see as how it's made any great difference. Run along now and look at the books as you please."

"Yes, ma'am," Lionel said.

The two friends moved off into still greater realms of mystery and adventure. Lionel pointed out more books to Ulysses. "These," he said. "And those over there. And these. All books, Ulysses." He stopped a moment to think. "I wonder what they say in all these books." He pointed out a whole vast area of them, five shelves full of them. "All these," he said—"I wonder what they say." Finally he discovered a book that looked very pretty from the outside. Its cover was green, like fresh grass. "And this one," he said, "this one is pretty, Ulysses."

A little frightened at what he was doing, Lionel lifted the book out of the shelf, held it in his hands a moment and then opened it. "There, Ulysses!" he said. "A book! There it is! See? They're saying something in here." Now he pointed to something in the print of the book. "There's an 'A,'" he said. "That's an 'A' right there. There's another letter of some sort. I don't know what that one is. Every letter's different, Ulysses, and every word's different." He sighed and looked around at all the books. "I don't think I'll ever learn to read," he said, "but I sure would like to know what they're saying in there. Now here's a picture," he said. "Here's a picture of a girl. See her? Pretty, isn't she?" He turned many pages of the book and said, "See it? More letters and words, straight through to the end of the book. This is the pubalic liberry, Ulysses," he said. "Books all over the place." He looked at the print of the book with a kind of reverence, whispering to himself as if he were trying to read. Then he shook his head. "You can't know what a book says, Ulysses, unless you can read, and I can't read," he said.

He closed the book slowly, put it back in its place, and together the two friends tiptoed out of the library. Outside, Ulysses kicked up his heel because he felt good, and because it seemed he had learned something new.[...]

CHAPTER 8   *A Letter from Marcus to His Brother Homer*

This Saturday was one of the longest and most eventful days of Homer Macauley's life. Little things began to take on fresh importance and to mean something which he could understand. The sleep of last night, troubled and full of grief, was now forever a part of his wakefulness. He had tried with all his might to keep the

messenger of Death from reaching Ithaca and its people. He had
dreamed that, but now it was no longer a dream.

The letter from his brother Marcus was with him, unopened,
waiting to be read.

He came into the telegraph office, limping, tired and eager to
rest. He looked at the call sheet and there were no calls to take. He
looked on the incoming telegram hook and there were no
telegrams to deliver.

His work was done. All was clear. He went to the old telegraph
operator and said, "Mr. Grogan, would you like to chip in with me
tonight for two day-old pies—apple and cocoanut cream?"

The old telegraph operator was by this time more than half
drunk. "I'll chip in, boy," he said, "but I'll not have any of the pies—
thanks just the same."

"If *you* don't want any of the pies, Mr. Grogan," Homer said, "I
don't want any either. I thought *you* might be hungry. I'm not hungry at all. I haven't had a chance to take it easy all day until now.
But I'm not hungry. It seems funny. You'd think a fellow would get
hungry working all day and all night, but he doesn't. I had a bowl
of chili at six tonight and that's all."

"How's your leg?" Grogan said.

"O.K.," Homer said. "I've forgotten all about it. I get around all
right." He looked curiously at the old telegraph operator and then
said very softly, "Are you drunk, Mr. Grogan?" He spoke earnestly
and the old man was not offended or hurt.

"Yes, I am, boy," Mr. Grogan said. He went to his chair and sat
down. After a moment he looked over at the boy across the table
from him, not sitting but standing there. "I feel a lot better when
I'm drunk," the old telegraph operator said. Then he brought the
bottle out and took a good long drink. "I'm not going to tell you
never to take a drink," he said. "I'm not going to say, as so many old
fools do—*Learn a lesson from me. Look what drink did to me*—that
would be a lot of nonsense. You're getting around now, seeing a lot
of things—a lot of things you never saw before. Well, let me tell you
something. Anything that concerns people—be very careful about
it. If you see something you're sure is wrong, don't be sure. If it's
people, be very careful. Now, you'll forgive me, but I must tell you,
because you're a man I respect, so I don't mind trying to tell you

that it's not right, it's foolish, to criticize the way any people happen to be. I haven't the slightest idea who you are—where you're from—how you came about—what made you the way you are—but I feel pleased about these things and I'm grateful. As a man gets closer to the end of his time he feels more and more grateful for the good people who're going to go on when he's gone. I might not be telling you this if I weren't drunk, so that alone is a good example of why it's wrong to have ideas about people who do things that everyone likes to feel aren't right. It's very important for me to tell you these things and for you to know them. Therefore, it is a good thing that I *am* drunk and that I am telling you. Can you understand what I'm saying?"

"I'm not sure, Mr. Grogan," Horner said.

"I'm telling you," the old telegraph operator said, "something that may embarrass you. And I could not tell you unless I were drunk. I'm telling you this—be grateful for yourself. Yes, for *yourself*. Be thankful. Understand that what a man is is something he *can* be grateful for, and *ought* to be grateful for, because if he is good, his goodness is not his alone, it's mine too, and the other fellow's. It's his only to protect and to spread around for me and for everybody else in the world. What you have is good, so be thankful for it. It will be welcomed by everyone you meet at one time or another. They will know you the minute they see you."

Now for some reason Homer remembered the girl at Bethel Rooms and the way she spoke to him, and as he remembered the old telegraph operator went on.

"They will know that you will not betray them or hurt them. They will know that you will not despise them after the whole world has despised them. They will know that you will see in them what the world has failed to see. You must know about that. You must not be embarrassed by it. You are a great man, fourteen years old. Who has made you great, nobody knows, but as it is true, know that it is true, be humble before it, and protect it. Do you understand?"

The messenger was extremely embarrassed, and it was very difficult for him to say, "I guess so, Mr. Grogan."

The old telegraph operator went on: "Then, I thank you. I have watched you, sober and drunk, since you came to work here, and, sober *or* drunk, I have recognized you. I have worked in cities in every part of the world. In my youth I wanted to reach many cities, and I reached them. All my life I have watched for you everywhere I have gone, and I have found you in many places—many out-of-the-way places—in many unknown people. I have found *something* of you in every man I have ever met, but most often it has not been enough. Now, in Ithaca, on my way home, I have found you again, better than ever, greater than ever. So, if you understand, I thank you. What is that you're holding—a letter? I have finished. Go ahead. Read your letter, boy."

"It's a letter from my brother Marcus," Homer said. "I haven't had a chance to open it yet."

"Then open it," the old telegraph operator said. "Read the letter from your brother. Read it aloud."

"Would you like to hear it, Mr. Grogan?" Homer said.

"Yes, if I may, I would like very much to hear it," the old telegraph operator said, and then took another drink.

Homer Macauley tore open the envelope of the letter from his brother Marcus, brought out the letter, unfolded it, and began to read, speaking very slowly.

"Dear Homer:" he read. "First of all, everything of mine at home is yours—to give to Ulysses when you no longer want them: my books, my phonograph, my records, my clothes when you're ready to fit into them, my bicycle, my microscope, my fishing tackle, my collection of rocks from Piedra, and all the other things of mine at home. They're yours rather than Bess's as you are now the man of the Macauley family of Ithaca. The money I made last year at the packing house I have given to Ma of course, to help out. It is not nearly enough, though, and soon Ma and Bess will be thinking of going to work. I cannot ask you not to allow them to go to work, but I am hoping that you yourself will not allow them to do so. I believe that you will not, as I know I would not. Ma would want to go to work, of course, and so would Bess. But that is all the more reason for you not to let them. I don't know how you are going to be able to keep our family together and go to high school at the same time, but I believe you will find a way. My Army pay goes to Ma, except for a few dollars that I must have, but this money is not enough. It is not easy for me to hope for so much from you, when I myself did not begin to work until I was nineteen, but somehow I believe that you will be able to do what I could not do.

"I miss you of course and I think of you all the time. I am happy, and even though I have never believed in wars—and know them to be foolish, even when they are necessary—I am proud that I am serving my country—which to me is Ithaca, our home, and all of the Macauleys. I do not recognize any enemy which is human, for no human being can be my enemy. Whoever he is, whatever color he is, however mistaken he may be in what he believes, he is my friend, not my enemy, for he is no different from myself. My quarrel is not with *him,* but with that in him which I seek to destroy in myself first.

"I do not feel like a hero. I have no talent for such feelings. I hate no one. I do not feel patriotic either, for I have always loved my country, its people, its towns, my home, and my family. I would rather I were not in the Army. I would rather there were no War, but as I *am* in the Army and as there is a War, I have long since made up my mind to be the best soldier it is possible for me to be. I have no idea what is ahead, but whatever it is I am humbly ready for it. I am terribly afraid—I must tell *you* this—but I know that when the time comes I shall do what is expected of me, and maybe even more than what is expected of me, but I want you to know I shall be obeying no command other than the command of my own heart. With me will be boys from all over America, from thousands of towns like Ithaca. I may be killed in this War. I must come right out and tell you this. I don't like the idea at all. More than anything else in the world I want to come back to Ithaca, and spend many long years with you and with my mother and sister and brother. I want to come back for Mary and a home and a family of my own. It is very likely that we shall be leaving soon—for action. Nobody knows where the action will be, but it is understood that we shall soon be leaving. Therefore, this may be my last letter to you for some time. I hope it is not the last of all. If it is, hold us together. Do not believe I am gone. Do not let the others believe it. My friend here is an orphan—a foundling—it is very strange that of all the boys here *he* should become my friend. His name is Tobey George. I have told him about Ithaca and our family. Some day I shall bring him to Ithaca with me. When you read this letter, do not be unhappy. I am glad that I am the Macauley who is in the War, for it would be a pity and a mistake if it were you.

"I can write to you what I could never say in words. You are the best of the Macauleys. You must go on being the best. Nothing must ever stop you. You are fourteen years old, but you must live to be twenty and then thirty and forty and fifty and sixty. You must live, in the years of your life, forever. I believe you will. I shall always be watching you. You are what we are fighting the War for. Yes, *you*—my brother. How could I ever tell you such things if we were together? You would jump on me and wrestle with me and call me a fool, but even so everything I have said is true. Now I will write your name here, to remind you: Homer Macauley. That's who you are. I miss you very much. I can't wait until I see you again. When that happens, when we meet again, I will let you wrestle me and put me down on my back in the parlor in front of Ma and Bess and Ulysses and maybe Mary even—I'll let you do that because I will be so glad to see you again. God bless you. So long. Your brother, Marcus."

While he was reading the letter the messenger sat down. He read very slowly, gulping many times, and becoming sick many times as he had been sick first in the house of the Mexican mother and then the night that he had cried while riding his bicycle around Ithaca after work. Now he got up. His hands were trembling. He bit the corner of his lip and looked over at the old telegraph operator, who was as deeply moved by the letter as the messenger himself. He spoke very softly. "If my brother is killed in this stupid War," he said, "I shall spit at the world. I shall hate it forever. I won't be good. I shall be the worst of them all, the worst that ever lived."

He stopped suddenly and tears came to his eyes. He hurried to the locker behind the repeater rack, took off his uniform and got into his regular clothes. He was running out of the office almost before his clothes had been properly arranged.

The old telegraph operator sat a long time. It was very quiet when he shook himself at last, finished the rest of the bottle, got up and looked around the office.

from *The Adventures of*
Wesley Jackson

CHAPTER 1 *Wesley Sings Valencia and Gets an Important Letter*
My name is Wesley Jackson, I'm nineteen years old, and my favorite
song is *Valencia.* I guess everybody in the world gets himself a favorite
song sometime or other. I know I've got mine because I keep singing
it or hearing it all the time, even in my sleep. I like the way the fellow
hollers at the top of his voice:

> *Valencia!*
> *In my dreams*
> *It always seems*
> *I hear you softly calling me!*
> *Valencia!*
> *Dat tarrata*
> *Dat tarrata*
> *Dat tarrata, dat ta ta!*

You can't get away from songs in this world because there's
always some kind of trouble going on in everybody and trouble
goes with singing. My pal Harry Cook sings *If I had my way, dear,*
you'd never grow old. He sings it to people he doesn't like, and he
means if he had his way they'd be dead, he doesn't mean he wants
them to stay young forever. At the same time he sings the song as if
he meant it the way the writer of the song meant it—as if he were
singing it to his bride and was broken-hearted because he couldn't
keep her young and pretty forever. But the man Harry's sore at
knows what Harry means, only he can't do anything about it

because it's a clean song and nobody could ever prove that Harry wasn't singing it to the girl who is going to be his bride some day. There's no law against singing to your sweetheart.

Nick Cully sings:

> *O Lord, you know I have no friend like you—*
> *Heaven's not my home, O Lord, what will I do?*
> *Angels beckon me to Heaven's open door*
> *And I can't feel at home in this world any more.*

Nick sings his song two ways too—serious and kidding. From the way Nick sings you know he means, "I don't like this life," but at the same time you know he also means, "I don't like it, but I want to keep it, so if I've *got* to go, for God's sake, let me go to a better place than this place—let me go to Heaven." You know Nick's homesick for some kind of impossible life, and you know he's making fun of his homesickness. Every time I hear Nick sing that song or remember his singing it, I get so sad I wish I was somebody else instead of who I am. I wish I was a Chinaman or an Eskimo or anything except what I am—an American born in San Francisco whose mother came from Dublin, whose father came from London, met in San Francisco, fell in love, got married and had two sons, myself and my brother Virgil. I get sick of my life when I hear Nick Cully asking the Lord what will he do if Heaven isn't his home, either.

Everybody I know has a song that he remembers from somewhere, that means something special to him. I like to wonder what kind of songs famous men sing to themselves when nobody's around. What a man sings in church is one thing and what he sings when he's alone is another.

So far you know my name, my age, and my favorite song, but you don't know the most important thing about me there is to know: I'm ugly. I'm not a *little* ugly like some fellows. I'm *all* ugly. Why this is so I don't know, but it's so and that's the end of it. Every time I go to shave I get a surprise. I can't believe *anybody* could be so ugly, but there he is right in front of my own eyes, and it's *me!* It's Wesley Jackson (39, 339, 993), it's not somebody else. I didn't know how ugly I was until I started to shave three years ago and had to look at myself every two or three days, and that's what I've got against shaving. I don't mind doing it, I don't mind trying to get neat, but I've got to look at myself when I shave and what I see makes me so sick I don't even bother to wish I was an Eskimo, I wish I was dead.

On account of this I took it into my head three years ago to stay out of sight as much as possible. I took long walks and read a lot of books. Walking gets you to thinking and reading puts you in touch with the thoughts of other men—most of them ugly men too, most likely. After you walk a lot and read a lot and think a lot you get to talking to yourself, only it isn't exactly to *yourself*, it's to the fellows you came to meet in the books. Pretty soon you get a hankering to talk to somebody alive, but when you go to do it, well, they don't know what you're talking about because they haven't been reading the books you've been reading or thinking the things you've been thinking, and chances are they think you're crazy. Maybe you are, but who knows who's crazy and who isn't? I wouldn't take it upon myself to say any man was crazy. I might be mistaken.

Next, you go to thinking you ought to write a letter to somebody, and that's what I did. I mean I *thought* I ought to write a letter, only I didn't know who to send it to. Mom had been separated from Pop most of my life, and I'd gotten out of touch with her.

As for Pop—hell, I didn't know where Pop was. As for my brother Virgil—what could you tell a fellow only thirteen years old even if you knew him, which I didn't? If I wrote to the President, wouldn't *he* be surprised?

I didn't know anybody else well enough to write to, so at last I wrote to Mrs. Fawkes who used to teach Sunday School in San Francisco.

Pop made me go to Sunday School because he claimed he'd lost the way to the good life and was afraid I'd lose it too if I didn't get a little assistance from somebody. He said it was up to me to find the way for the two of us, but hell, *Pop* was the drunkard, not me. *He* should have gone to Sunday School.

I wrote to Mrs. Fawkes a long letter and told her some of the things that had happened to me since I had seen her last which was nine years ago. I didn't think she would remember me, but it seemed to me I ought to write to somebody, so I wrote to her. What's the use being in the Army if you don't write a letter once in a while and get one back once in a while? If Mrs. Fawkes wrote back, O.K. If she didn't, O.K.

One night about a month after I had sent my letter to Mrs. Fawkes there was a big commotion at Mail Call because there was a letter for me. Vernon Higbee started the fuss. Instead of throwing the letter to me the way he did for everybody else, he said he wanted to present it to me officially. The boys liked the idea of making it official and I didn't mind particularly, so when they made a path for me to the platform, I walked down the path and up onto the platform beside Vernon, the way they expected me to do it. I knew they wanted to have a little fun and when a lot of fellows in the Army want to have a little fun the best thing to do is let them, because if you don't, they have *more* fun, and you don't have any at all. But if you let them, then you have a little fun yourself. If people laugh at you, who are they laughing at? I laugh at myself, why shouldn't a lot of fellows in the Army laugh at me too? Everybody learns to laugh at himself after the age of eighteen, I guess.

Well, when I got up onto the platform beside Vernon everybody was laughing and having fun, so Vernon stretched his arm out the way public speakers do who've got control over their audience.

"Quiet, everybody!" he said. "This is the most important occasion of my career as Mail Clerk of Company B. I have the honor to announce that a letter has come through the American Postal System—and I have the further and greater honor to announce that this letter is addressed to Private Wesley Jackson. Three cheers for Private Jackson please."

The fellows cheered and I kept wondering what Mrs. Fawkes had to say in the letter. At the same time I kept hearing the fellow hollering *Valencia*.

After the cheers somebody said, "Who's the letter from?" And somebody else said, "Don't tell us even Wesley's got a girl."

But I didn't care.

"One thing at a time please," Vernon Higbee said. "With Private Jackson's kind permission I will tell you who the letter is from. As to the matter of whether or not Private Jackson has a girl, the affirmative or the negative of that circumstance is not involved in this ceremony which is official. The letter I hold in my hand, which is the private property of Private Jackson, is very clearly addressed to him by title, which is Private, by name, which is Wesley Jackson, and by Army Serial Number, which is 39, 339,993—all in accordance with Army Regulations. Three cheers for Army Regulations."

The fellows cheered the Army Regulations, and then Vernon said, "Now. Who is the letter from? The letter is from the Seventh Avenue Presbyterian Church of San Francisco." Here Vernon turned to me.

"Private Jackson," he said, "I take great pleasure in presenting to you on behalf of the Nation this letter which has come to you from the Seventh Avenue Presbyterian Church of San Francisco, a city close to my heart, only nine miles across the bay from my own home in San Leandro, and almost two hundred miles from this Army Post."

Vernon clicked his heels and came to attention. For some reason every one of the fellows standing around waiting for their own mail, about a hundred of them, did the same thing. They didn't follow Vernon's *example*, they clicked their heels and came to attention *with* him, the way a flock of sparrows will fly from a telegraph wire together. It was a game, but I didn't mind at all. I even liked it a little because I never saw those fellows so smart before, not even on parade. If it's for fun, a fellow can do almost anything in a smart way. Besides, Mrs. Fawkes had answered my letter and pretty soon I'd be reading it.

Vernon bowed, handed me my letter, and everybody roared with a kind of laughter you don't hear anywhere except in the Army, or maybe in a penitentiary. I could still hear them laughing as I ran to the woods I used to go to when I was at that Post. When I got to the woods I sat down under a tree and put the letter on the ground in front of me and looked at it.

It was the first letter I had ever gotten in my life, and my name and everything was typed out on the envelope, *oh Valencia!*

After a while I opened the envelope to see what Mrs. Fawkes had to say, but the letter wasn't from Mrs. Fawkes, it was from the preacher of the church. He said he was sorry to tell me that Mrs. Fawkes was dead. She had passed on in her sleep three months ago, aged 71. He said he had taken the liberty of opening my letter, and he said he had read it a half dozen times. I was a fine Christian young man (which was something I never knew until he told me and something Pop would be glad to hear). He said he was going to pray for me and he told me to pray too—but he didn't tell me to pray for *him*. He said a lot of other things that I read while the tears came out of my eyes because Mrs. Fawkes was dead, and then he said, "There is one thing I have decided after careful consideration to tell you, which I hope you will have the courage to accept with dignity and resignation: *You are a writer.* I have been writing for the better part of forty years, and I must say that even though my work has not gone altogether unheeded (I published a small inspirational book fifteen years ago at my own expense called *Smiling Through in Spite of the Tears* which Reverend R. J. Featherwell of Sausalito, California, used as the subject of a sermon in which he said, 'Here is a book the world has long been waiting for—a book whose gentle light a dark and evil world stands very much in need of')—even though, as I say, my work has not gone altogether unheeded, I must tell you that your writing is better than mine, therefore you must write. Write, my boy!"

Well, I thought the man must be foolish, but after a while I found myself taking his advice, and that's how it happens that I am writing this story which is about myself mainly, since I don't know anybody else very well, but about others too as far as I know them.

I was pretty careful of my language in my letter to Mrs. Fawkes—and my thoughts too, I guess—but I don't have to be careful any more and I mean to say what I think is right at the time, no matter what it comes to.

CHAPTER 2   *Wesley Explains What the Army Does to a Fellow, Says Something He Thinks Is Right, and Can't Sleep*

I said the letter I got from the preacher in answer to my letter to Mrs. Fawkes was the only letter I ever got in my life, but that isn't quite the truth, although it's not a lie either. I got a letter from the President once, but I don't think he knew very much about it, so I didn't count it. It wasn't personal anyway. It didn't seem sincere either. I read the word *Greetings* and wondered why it wasn't *Goodbye*, considering it meant I was going to be in the Army very soon. I'd heard that if you could breathe, the Army wanted you, and

I used to breathe just fine. I'd heard a lot of other things about the
Army, some of them funny and some of them dirty, but all they
ever came to was that I'd soon be in uniform because I had no criminal record, I wasn't insane, I didn't have a weak heart, my blood
pressure was fine, and I had all the fingers and toes and eyes and
ears and different things I was born with, all of them O.K. It seemed
as if I had been cut out to be a soldier all the time and was only
hanging around the Beach and the Public Library in San Francisco
waiting for the declaration of War. All the same, I wasn't raring to
go. I was raring *not* to go.

One or two times I thought I'd hide away in the hills somewhere
and wait for the War to end. One time I even got the stuff I'd need
for a life like that and tied it up into a bundle and took a street-car
as far out of town as I could go. I got out on the Great Highway and
a fellow gave me a ride sixty miles south to Gilroy, but when I
looked around I was still in the same country and everybody was
still excited about the War. Everybody seemed sick with the excitement, and the excitement seemed obscene. I bought a hamburger
and a cup of coffee, and then I hitch-hiked home. I didn't tell a soul
what I'd done. I didn't even mention how I'd looked over my shoulder at the Coast Range Mountains where I thought I'd go to live
during the War and felt so lonely and helpless and ignorant and
cheap and disgraceful that I began to hate the whole world, which
is something I don't like to do because the world is people and people are too pathetic to hate. I just moved along with everybody else,
and when the time came I went down to 444 Market Street and got
took into the Army.

But that's all ancient history now, and I don't propose to fool
with any ancient history in this story. Some day this whole War is
going to be ancient history and I am going to want to know what
the consensus of opinion is going to be about it then. I am going to
want to be interested in the outcome. I wouldn't be a bit surprised
if this War turned out to be the turning point, as they say on the
radio. The trouble is if you think about a turning point three or
four minutes you come to the conclusion that there is nothing
in the world that *isn't* a turning point, and the only thing that's
important about a turning point is what it's a turning point from,

and what it's a turning point to. If it's a turning point from nothing to nothing, what good is it? Maybe it might have been ignored even, although I can't see how anybody who isn't lame or mad can ignore a War, considering the mail he gets and the complications that come into his life once he's opened the mail and looked at it.

I remember before the War started that nobody in the whole country knew I was alive or cared much one way or the other. Nobody invited me to pitch in and help solve the problems of peace. And yet I was always the same fellow and always in need of a little ready cash. That's why the big-family spirit that comes over a whole country when there's a War makes me a little suspicious of the people who throw the party because it seems to me they are always smiling and full of hope and too quick to be heroic, whereas the fellows in uniform are confused and miserable most of the time and only begin to smile when there's nothing else to do, and are never terribly hopeful because they don't know very much about what's going on or what it means or what the outcome is likely to be—for themselves, I mean—and never in a hurry to be heroic because with a little bad luck they might be both heroic and dead. And when a fellow knows a thing like that he can't enjoy a party with all his heart and soul. Henry Rhodes used to say when he and I were at the Reception Center together for the first few days of our life in the Army, "This is the bum's rush, Jackson, and you and I are a couple of the bums."

Henry Rhodes was a Certified Public Accountant who worked in an office on Montgomery Street in San Francisco until he was drafted. He was no kid. He was forty-three years old, but in those days they took them all.

I said I was going to say whatever I think is right, no matter what it is. Well, the time has come for me to say something that I think is right, but here I am scared to death to say it. *I'm* scared because I'm in the Army, but what the hell's scaring the people who aren't in the Army? The minute a War starts everybody seems to forget everything he ever knew—everything that's worth a hoot—and shuts his mouth and keeps it shut and just groans with agony about the lies he hears all over the place all the time.

From the beginning they scare you to death in the Army. They begin scaring you with the *Articles of War*. They don't mean to be human about any of the difficulties a fellow is apt to get into, they just naturally threaten to kill you, that's all. They tell you so while you're lifting your arm to take the oath. They tell you before your arm is down, before you're *in* the Army, "—the punishment is Death." They are your own family, the same people who tell you so many other things, so many of them so confusing after you've been told what the punishment is. Of course they hardly ever have to give a fellow that punishment, but the word Death is forever after hanging around in the whole idea of Army law and order, and pretty soon it seeps down into every little irritating rule it's possible for a fellow to break, so that if he goes to get a drink of water in the afternoon they call it Absent Without Leave, which is very serious, and for which the punishment, although called Extra Duty, is actually Death. Or if he lets the tap water run while he's washing instead of filling the basin, again the punishment is Extra Duty, but that's just another term for Murder as far as I'm concerned. You get six or seven months of that kind of law and order and if you aren't scared to death, or full of confusion and anger, you're a better man than I am because even though I'm easy-going about all things, and by rights shouldn't be scared or confused or angry, I am scared, I am confused, I am angry. I don't like it, but I just can't help it.

Anyway, I was talking about Henry Rhodes and the thing I felt I ought to say about him because I felt it was right but was afraid to say because I am in the Army was this: Henry Rhodes was sore at the government for drafting him into the Army.

I was afraid to say a little thing like that.

I'm ashamed of myself.

I can't sleep from thinking about these things, but sometimes when I can't sleep it's on account of the noise the fellows make in the barracks all night, talking, telling dirty stories, singing, or playing games on each other, like the game Dominic Tosca and Lou Marriacci play on Dominic's brother Victor who sleeps in the bunk between them.

As soon as Victor falls asleep Dominic on one side and Lou on the other start whispering in his ear: "I don't want to be in the Army. Why did this happen to me? I was minding my own business. I don't want to be a soldier. I don't want to kill anybody. I want to go home. I don't want to die." They whisper louder and louder until poor Victor wakes up and says, "Ah cut it out, will you? I'm going to tell Mama on you Dominic." All the fellows in the barracks roar with laughter, even me, and I don't think it's funny at all.[...]

CHAPTER 8   *Wesley Studies the Various Groups in the German Prison Camp*

Victor and I stayed captured by the Germans until the last day of August when they went off and left us. We saw a lot of stuff in that Prison Camp—some of it funny and wonderful and beautiful, and some of it terrible and ugly. The Germans didn't say anything to us when they left. They just packed up in the night and went off, and the next day we waited and waited, but the Germans were gone. There were over a thousand of us cooped up inside barbed-wire, and we'd been there a long time, so when it got around that the Germans had gone and left us—well, we turned into a mob.

Victor and I had met in that Prison Camp the day before the Fourth of July, so we had been there together almost two months. The Fourth of July was celebrated, but not very successfully. Somebody tried to put on a show, but it didn't work. When a fellow got up to make a speech everybody told him to skip it. They were rude to the fellow, who had only meant to do something right. The show was supposed to be a kind of stage show—a little vaudeville— but nobody wanted to bother with it, so after a half hour it fell to pieces and everybody went back to waiting.

I'll mention the terrible things first and get them out of the way. One night a boy cut his wrists and was found dead in the morning.

And one afternoon two paratroopers who had been pals got irritated with one another because one of them said a certain girl they both knew had been had by six of their friends (not counting themselves) and the other said she had been had by only five. The sixth was also a paratrooper but a fellow one of them hated, so he didn't want that paratrooper to have had the girl too. His pal kept saying that he *knew* he had had her too, so the fellow who said the girl had been had by only five took his pal by the throat and began to choke him. But his pal had been taught a few things about hand-to-hand fighting too, so they almost killed each other. When they had been separated they agreed through the fellows speaking for them that one of them would stay on one side of the stockade and the other on the other, because they insisted that if they ever met again they would kill each other—and they meant it too, although they had been pals and had been through a lot of campaigns together. They kept their word, and each of them stayed on his side of the stockade. They never spoke to each other again.

There were a half dozen little fights every day because everybody was so tense, but the fight between the paratroopers was the only serious one.

The fellows divided up into little groups which were held together by the ties that have always made men feel related.

For the most part, fellows who had been in the same outfit stuck together because they had the same things to remember and talk about.

Then there were little groups that were held together because the fellows came from the same city and liked to talk about home or people they remembered.

Then there were groups that were formed because the fellows had had the same trades or professions in civilian life and liked to talk over the circumstances of their work in the past and prospects for the future.

Then there were regional groups. Southerners liked to stay together because they felt the same way about Negroes—and Negroes liked to stay together because they knew how the Southerners felt, or didn't want to be bothered. There were only nine Negroes in the stockade. Only three of them were Southern and weren't college graduates but the other six were fond of the three who weren't as educated as they were.

Fellows from the Far West—California, Oregon and Washington—felt close together.

Then there were fellows who happened to have the same last name. Sometimes there would be only two and the name would be unusual and they would try to understand how they had come to have that name—Menadue—and yet weren't related and didn't know the same people.

Or there would be two fellows—one from Tennessee and the other from North Dakota—whose last name was Rosevar. They would take up with one another and talk about their families and get to be pals because their names were so unusual, and yet they weren't related.

There were seven Smiths, and they called each other Smithy, and so did everybody else. The four or five Browns got along nicely and were often together.

Then, fellows with the same temperament seemed to like hanging around together—comedians especially, but a lot of fellows who were serious-minded stayed together too.

Fellows feeling homesick would hang around a lot, but as soon as the feeling was gone they'd go back to another group. As soon as they weren't quite as homesick as they'd been, they'd take up with the sporting crowd, for instance, which was always busy with little athletics that didn't require running or a lot of space: Indian wrestling, standing broad jump, distance spitting, and stuff like that.

Or they'd take up with the prophesying group and prophesy this and that.

Or they'd take up with the dreamers—fellows who lived to discuss what romantic things they were going to do after the War.

As soon as a fellow with a cold got over his cold he'd leave his pals with colds and go along to one or another of the other groups, such as the discussers of current events, politics, religion, Communism, or philosophy.

Then there were size groups: little men, medium-sized men, and big men.

Or appearance groups: handsome men, not quite handsome men, plain men, or strange-looking men.

Then there were personality groups.

Fellows with a long record of conquests liked to hang around together and compare notes and go over each success in detail.

Fellows with the attitude that women are meant to be stalked and taken like any other animal not easy to stalk and take enjoyed one another's company.

Fellows who believed their wives were lonely worried about them and stayed together.

Fellows who felt sure their wives hadn't been true to them after so much separation spent a lot of time together wondering whether they ought to get divorced, forgive and forget, or catch the son of a bitch (or the several of them) who took their wives away from them while their backs were turned and they were fighting the War. But even among themselves these fellows were divided because some of them sympathized with their wives. The fellows who didn't sympathize with their wives would be irritated with the fellows who did and would consider them poor specimens of manhood, and the talk would get pretty heated and confused sometimes.

Then there were the fellows who had had very few women.

And the ones who had had none—but this group was very small because they were shy about it.

Then there were those who probably hadn't had any women, but liked to say they had, and understood one another and got along all right.

Then there were the men with one child, and the men with two, and the handful with three or more. The man with seven children—Orin Oakley, of Kentucky—belonged to no group at all. He just sat and invented names for famous men. One of the best was Rearview Mirror.

Then there were the men who went after women a lot, but admitted they hated them and only liked to bring them down a peg, especially the proud ones—make them fall in love and then let them suffer. These men liked to discuss the pitiable conditions to which they had reduced many a vain hussy—made them humiliate themselves; made them write letters, send telegrams, telephone all the time; made them leave their husbands; made whores out of them; made them beg to be loved; made them go mad, and so on and so forth.

Then there were groups made up of cynics—fellows who were sure the world was shot to hell for good, and hated humanity because it stank.

Then there were the laughers; the moaners; the travelers; the stay-at-homes; the foolish; the wise; the gamblers; the readers; the chess crowd; the dice boys.

There were all kinds, but no matter how they broke themselves up, they were all one thing; prisoners.

They were captured by the Germans, and they were captured by the Americans—and they didn't like being captured by anybody.

CHAPTER 9   *John Wynstanley of Cincinnati, Ohio, Puts on a*
                Strawhat and Plays the Trombone, Enchanting
                Enemy and Friend Alike

There was a fellow in the stockade named John Wynstanley who had
a trombone. He'd carried it with him from his home in Cincinnati,
and he'd kept it in the War two years. He was a little bit of a fellow
with a grave preoccupied expression on his face. He didn't look more
than sixteen or seventeen years old, although he was past twenty.

Everybody knew he had a trombone, but Wynstanley wouldn't
bring it out of the case and play it because he said he couldn't play
it unless he had a strawhat on his head. He had always had a
strawhat, and he'd brought it to France with him, but somebody
had stolen it.

If somebody would get him a strawhat, he'd play the trombone.

Well, nobody had a strawhat, so the only thing to do was take the
matter up with the Germans. There were three or four of our fellows who could speak German, so one of them told the Guards
what was needed, but the Guards said they didn't have a strawhat.
They said they'd like to hear somebody play the trombone all right,
but where would they be able to get a strawhat?

The Guards were told to scout around, and tell their friends, and
see if they couldn't find a strawhat somewhere because Wynstanley
couldn't play the trombone until he had a strawhat on his head.
Maybe he really knew how to play the trombone, and if he did, it
would be worth it.

The Guards said they would look into the matter.

After a while everybody decided Wynstanley couldn't play the
trombone. They decided he had invented the story about the
strawhat, so he could get out of being exposed.

Wynstanley prided himself on being a good trombone-player,
and he didn't like the slur, so on the evening of Sunday, July 9th, he
brought the trombone out of the case and put it together. Everybody
gathered around and waited—at least three hundred fellows.

Wynstanley wet his lips and pressed them against the mouth-
piece and slided the trombone back and forth a couple of times to
get it moving smoothly.

Then he began to play something that just about brought heaven into that miserable place. But, sure enough, he stopped playing and said, "Got to have a strawhat on my head—can't play worth a damn without a strawhat."

So then everybody knew he wasn't kidding. They ran over to the Guards and told them for God's sake, send to Paris for a strawhat because this boy knows how to blow the trombone, so the Guards said yes, they had heard him and would try their best.

Nobody badgered Wynstanley to play the trombone without a strawhat on his head after that because there is something almost religious about a man who knows how to cope with a horn, especially a trombone, and is able to bring music out of it. Everybody had a lot of respect for Wynstanley for having lugged the trombone half across the world, and after he had played enough to let everybody know he wasn't bluffing, they knew this wasn't any ordinary fellow, this was somebody special, and the only thing to do was get him a strawhat.

Wynstanley showed some of the fellows a snapshot of himself when he was nine years old. He had a trombone to his lips and a strawhat on his head.

"Always wore a strawhat when I played," he said.

Well, the song Wynstanley had started to play that night was *You'll never know just how much I love you,* and hell, it was wonderful—it was just naturally out of the world—and he went on to *You'll never know just how much I care*—just as easy and heartbreaking as anything could be, but when he came to the next few bars, well, he just couldn't go on.

Instead of being impatient with him—instead of thinking he was affected or silly—everybody took to feeling sympathetic. They tried to comfort him, and they said, "That's all right, Johnny—you'll get your strawhat, and then you can really play." Everybody could see he *wanted* to play, but was too good to let himself play poorly.

Well, the days and nights dragged along and the groups formed and broke up and re-formed and changed and were abandoned and new groups came along. But everybody had all kinds of stuff going on inside himself that was all his own, and there was no grouping of that stuff at all.

And everybody knew John Wynstanley was there with his trombone. Everybody had heard enough of the song he had started to play to want him to finish it, but nobody tried to rush him into doing a poor job.

One day one of the Guards told one of our fellows who knew German that according to some gossip he'd heard another Guard was returning from leave in Paris, and he was bringing a strawhat with him.

So everybody got happy about that and the news was carried to Wynstanley.

"When's he coming with it?" Wynstanley said.

"Any day now," somebody said. "Does it have to be any particular size?"

"It ought to fit," Wynstanley said, "but if it's straw and I can get it on my head, it'll do."

So then along with all the other waiting—waiting for the War to end, waiting to be captured back by the Americans, waiting to get to some place where we could get our mail—we started waiting for Wynstanley's strawhat to arrive.

Waiting's waiting and it's no trouble at all while you're waiting for a lot of important things to wait for a few unimportant ones too.

At last the fellow who'd been to Paris came back and sure enough, he'd brought a strawhat with him. He said he wanted to give it to Wynstanley himself. He came inside the stockade, and the fellows who spoke German walked along with him to Wynstanley who was sitting on the trombone case, the way he always sat. If he got up to walk, he carried the case with him by the handle. He took the thing with him wherever he went. Well, Wynstanley looked up at the German who'd been to Paris because the German was carrying a package and maybe there was a strawhat in it.

The interpreter said to Wynstanley, "He's brought you a strawhat from Paris—his name's Trott von Essen."

"Ask him," Wynstanley said, "can I keep the hat? I'll pay him what it cost and something for his trouble."

So the interpreter talked to Trott and then said to Wynstanley, "He says it's a pleasure—you can have the hat—glad to do it."

"Ask him," Wynstanley said, "what he'd like me to play because the first song I play has got to be for him—for getting me the hat."

So then the interpreter talked to Trott again, and then said to Wynstanley, "He says finish the song you started to play about two weeks ago."

"Tell him," Wynstanley said, "it's a deal and let's have a look at the hat."

So the interpreter told Trott, and Trott broke the string of the package and brought out a brand new strawhat with a red band on it, and a little cluster of red and green and purple feathers stuck in the band.

Trott handed Wynstanley the hat, and Wynstanley just held it and looked at it a long time.

Then he put it on his head.

It looked very good on him. He looked like a civilian all of a sudden.

Then very slowly Wynstanley opened the case and put the trombone together and slided it back and forth a couple of times. Then he went to work and played the song like nobody in the whole world had ever played it before.

It was the most magnificent thing anybody ever heard. He played it through three times, each time just a little better than the time before.

Wynstanley had been hungry to play and nobody needed to tell him to go on—he just *wanted* to play, and he did. It was the finest thing that happened in the whole War. Trott von Essen was so proud of his share in the event he would hardly talk to the interpreters.

Everybody had a favorite song he wanted to hear, and Wynstanley promised to play them all one after another—if he couldn't play them tonight, he'd play them tomorrow. If you could whistle or hum the tune, he'd pick it up and play it for you, he said. He didn't care what the tune was or whether he'd heard it before, just whistle it or hum it and he'd listen, and play it for you. He told the interpreter to ask Trott if there was any other song he'd like to hear, so Trott thought a minute, and remembered one, but didn't know the name of it. He'd heard one of our fellows singing it one night and he'd liked it, so Wynstanley told the interpreter to ask Trott to hum the song, or whistle it.

Trott hummed a few bars, and Wynstanley smiled and said, "Hell, that's *I'm thinking tonight of my blue eyes.* That's one of my own favorites."

Wynstanley played that song too, and if he was good on the first one, he was better on the second. The German was just as happy and proud as he could be. He wanted to know from the interpreter what the song was about, so the interpreter told him. He asked the interpreter to teach him to say *blue eyes* in English, so the interpreter did, and he went off saying the two words over and over again.

After *Blue Eyes,* Wynstanley played *Oh the moonlight's fair tonight along the Wabash, from the fields there comes the scent of newmown hay,* and damned if every fellow listening didn't have tears in his eyes and go to work and blow his nose and wonder how so much beauty could come out of a little old battered-up piece of plumbing like John Wynstanley's trombone.

I don't know what the fellows in the American Army are fighting for, or what they think they're fighting for, because I haven't asked every one of them, but I think I know what they love—every last one of them, no matter who they are or what group they belong to—they love truth and beauty. They love it and need it and want it and tears come to their eyes when they get it.

And they got it when John Wynstanley of Cincinnati, Ohio, played the trombone. They got it when that great American—that great man of the world—put the strawhat on his head and let them hear the message of love and truth and beauty.

And I don't know what's American as against what's something else, but I know there is no man in the world capable of resisting truth and beauty like the truth and beauty that came out of Wynstanley's trombone on the evening and night of Saturday, July 22, 1944.

I know the German Guards couldn't resist that truth and beauty, because, having got a hint of its enormity, one of them had fetched Wynstanley his strawhat. And I know the men named Rosevar and Menadue couldn't resist it; or the men named Smith or Jones; or the men who came from the South and had a special attitude toward Negroes; or the Negroes; or the fellows from the Far West; or the men who were cynics; or the ones who hated women; or the ones with toothaches; or those with colds; or the athletic ones; or the ones who despised the world; or those who had no religion; or the paratroopers. I know everybody in that Prison Camp and everybody outside of it who heard Wynstanley could not resist the truth and beauty he brought out of his trombone—and they were all the same in the presence of that truth and beauty, so what's all this talk about some people being no good by birth, and others being very good by birth, and others being fair to middling by birth? What kind of talk is that?

The Theological Student

I began to meet the theological student about a quarter of a century ago in the plays of certain Russian writers. Tolstoy, Dostoyevsky, Chekhov, Andreyev and Gorki seldom wrote a play in which the theological student did not appear. The theological student seemed to be the playwright himself looking back at his youth with an amused but admiring eye. He was certainly a good man to have around—young; nervous; pale; often pimply; not the least bit handsome; ridiculous and pathetic; ill-clothed; ill-fed; eager for tea; full of the lore of heaven, hell and earth; and yet for all that a man who could be counted on to liven matters up considerably, for he was a devil at heart.

He was certainly always in the midst of a desperate struggle with sin, which appeared to be an overwhelming longing to kiss the girls, a longing that never failed to startle him and bewilder them. Some of the girls were women with children older than himself. These rather liked him, for he was clumsy, inexperienced, inept, and therefore amusing to them. More in charity than in passion they permitted him to breathe heavily in their arms, only to discover later in the afternoon that he was thinking of killing himself. His habit of coughing nervously in their faces made them cry out, "Oh, Alexander Alexandrovich!"—which he took for an expression of love. He disgraced himself in company by his ill-timed remarks and by his uncontrollable desire to escape being good.

He was useful to each playwright, however, in that it seemed perfectly natural for him to explain why humanity was unhappy.

In the plays of Tolstoy the theological student blamed man's unhappiness on women, and sometimes went so far as to mention certain physical parts of them to which men were so powerfully attracted that they could not give their undivided attention to God or farming; and then, in another play, Tolstoy would have the theological student blaming something else.

Once, I believe it was the railroads, tempting men to run away. (From women of course, although the playwright mentioned only crying children and members of the local government who were forever greeting people in a most insincere manner.)

Another time the theological student, having had no stronger stimulant than a cup of tea, shouted that man is a beast because of his stomach; and went on to ask if anyone had recently noticed how frequently men sit down to eat, how much precious time is wasted in eating or in planning to do so, and what mischief attends the circumstance of a stomach full of meat, wheat, greens, cheese, wine and water.

Dostoyevsky's theological student claimed that man was unhappy because his very birth had been a nervous disorder.

 Gorki's theological student was the best of the lot, though, for he hated everything which made life miserable, and everything made life miserable. The theological student proceeded quite logically to find fault with God, whereupon another side of Gorki, embodied in another character in the play—a notorious waster of sixty who had recently read a book from cover to cover—came forward with an attack on the government, blaming it for his present age and ill-health, and remarking profoundly that he had once been thirty—no, even less than that—twenty! But now what? A ridiculous thing in a ridiculous black cloak! (Looking meaningfully across the room at Tatania Lvovna, age 18, and detecting in her the faintest trace of admiration.)

Having met the theological student and having found him an odd sort of fish—in no particular greatly different from anyone else I had met in the Russian plays—I began to wonder what it was that he was supposed to be studying. Whatever it was, did he study full-time or part-time? Did he study at school or at home? Or was he called a theological student simply because he was young? None of the playwrights was very clear about any of this, other than to hint that what the theological student *wanted* was perfection.

At length I decided for myself that he studied theology books, and I decided to do so also.

*   *   *

A whole small mezzanine balcony with a floor of thick glass was devoted to books of theology at the Public Library in Fresno. Climbing the steep narrow stairway to this section of the library was like climbing upward on a small cramped ship. Once there, the feeling of sailing was very great, and the faces of the other readers seemed flushed by a mild fever, as if they were all a little seasick and were trying their best not to throw up. They were certainly dizzy from the height, the hot air, and the narrowness of the aisles between the shelves of books. I joined them and began to examine every book on the theology shelves.

Every book seemed depressing, but I was fearful of putting one of them back in its place until I was reasonably sure it was absurd and did not have hidden away in it somewhere what I was looking for.

What *was* I looking for? It did not occur to me at the time—nothing much occurs to anybody at the time and we might as well come right out and admit it—but whether I knew it in so many words or not I was very definitely looking for a theology which I myself might have written, or might one day write. That is to say, I was looking for what I believed was the only true theology. Robert Burns had already summed it up with Scotch economy, but one frequently forgets the remarks of poets. "A man's a man for all that" was right enough, and the implication of laughing about it was in the remark, but I imagined there would be a fuller recitation on the theme.

There wasn't, however.

The millions of words in the hundreds of books were little more than nonsense. Even so, I took home with me after each visit two or three of the theology books which I felt might not prove to be altogether senseless, and read around in them until I was convinced that the author was as ridiculous as any theological student in any Russian play.

No writer is more pathetic than the one whose passion is to complicate, and theology appeared to be a matter of complicating. If it was a matter of believing, why not believe and be done with it? Swedenborg sweated like a horse and wrote a couple of million words that must have had the effect of making it impossible for any reader ever again to smile, itself a kind of theological act, although uncomplicated and surely no more meaningless than Swedenborg's two million words.

All of which brings me to the plot of this story.

One evening on my way home from the Public Library I was met in the Santa Fe freight yards by a man who was profoundly complicated and desperately theological.

"Do you know," he called out from a distance of twenty yards, "that the world is going to end tonight?"

"What time?" I called back.

"Don't know the exact hour," the man said, "but it will be sometime tonight."

From his shoulders the man brushed dirt which had gotten there when he had leaped from a freight train and fallen.

"Did you just get to town?" I said.

"Yes, but I was born here twenty-seven years ago," the man said.

"Are you ready for the end of the world?" he went on, as he took to brushing dust from his pants.

"As ready as I am for anything else," I said. "Are *you* ready?"

"That's the trouble," the man said. "I'm not. I'm not at all."

Suddenly the man fell down.

"Do you know where the Emergency Hospital is?" I said. "It's at the back of the Police Station on Broadway, across from the Public Library, but if you don't want to go there, you can go to the County Hospital. It's across Ventura Boulevard at the Fair Grounds, but I suppose you know where these places are. I live on the way to the County Hospital and I'll go with you as far as my house. Maybe you can pick up a ride."

The man leaned on me and we stumbled in silence past Inderrieden's Dried Fruit Packing House. Crossing Ventura he fell again, and an automobile stopped. The driver of the automobile got out and came to the man and said, "What's the matter?"

"He ought to get to a doctor," I said. "He's hurt."

The driver of the automobile helped me get the man into the car. On the way to the County Hospital the injured man took one of the three books I had borrowed from the Public Library and opened it.

"*Either-Or*," he read. "By Sören Kierkegaard. Who's he?"

"I don't know," I said.

"A man ought to know who these people are," the man said.

He began to read the book. When we reached the hospital his grip was so tight on the book that I felt sure it would be damaged and the girl at the desk in the Public Library would examine the damage, and then me, and wonder how it had happened, but not say anything.

The driver of the car—a man who had remarked on the way to the hospital that his name was August Bockbell, a name I have never forgotten, perhaps because the driver—sensing that the other man was dying—gave an account of his *own* life, which included almost killing his elder brother over the ownership of a pocket-knife—helped the injured man into the reception room, and then went off, apologizing that it was necessary for him to do so.

I did not go with him because the injured man was still reading the book I had borrowed from the Public Library, and it seemed to me that it would have been rude under the circumstances to ask him to return it. He was reading the book with incredible swiftness. When it was necessary for the injured man to go off with the nurse and a young man in a white coat who did not seem to be much of a doctor, I followed them down a hall to swinging doors, partly from anxiety about the man himself and partly from anxiety about the library book. At the swinging doors the nurse told me to return to the reception room. I wanted to ask her to please get my book for me, but instead I said, "He's going to be all right, isn't he?" The nurse gestured severely, as if to say, "No difficult questions at this difficult time, please."

I returned to the reception room and sat down.

When I examined the two remaining library books, I discovered that my library card with my name and address on it was in the book by Kierkegaard which the injured man had taken. My library card was as important to me as a passport is to a traveller. I had thought of waiting only ten or fifteen minutes for the book, but when I discovered that my library card was in it, I decided to wait two hours if necessary.

It was necessary to wait longer than that, however, during which time I grew very hungry—half-sick from it, in fact—and very angry, too. At first I was angry at the nurse who entered the reception room every ten or fifteen minutes in a state of confusion and excitement and refused to listen to what I had to tell her or to tell me about the condition of the injured man. After awhile I became angry about the man himself, whether he was to live or die—for he had most rudely taken off with a book I was charged on my honor to return to the Public Library in the same condition in which I had found it. Finally, I became angry about Kierkegaard, a man concerning whom I knew absolutely nothing except that he had written a book with the strange title of *Either-Or*.

After having waited more than three hours for the return of my book, the nurse came up to me in the reception room in a manner which revealed unmistakably that she meant to speak, and began by announcing a hopelessly garbled version of *my* name.

"Yes?" I said.

"He's dead," she went on. "Dr. Humpkit (at least that's what I *thought* she said) did everything possible for him, but it was just no use."

"I'm sorry. The thing I wanted to tell you was to please let me have my book."

"What book?"

"The book by Kierkegaard."

"He said it was *his* book. His library card with his *name* and *address* on it is in the book, at any rate."

"The card in the book is *my* card," I said. "Why do you get everything wrong? I was walking home from the Public Library with three books when I met the man in the Santa Fe freight yards. He had just jumped off a train and had hurt himself, so I helped him to Ventura Avenue where he fell down and a motorist stopped and brought him here. In the automobile he took one of the three books I had borrowed from the Public Library and kept it. Now he's dead, and just because my library card happened to be in the book, you've given *him* my name. Well, I'm sorry he's dead whoever he is, but I'd like to have my book back just the same."

"He himself told us his name," the nurse said. "I am entering it in the hospital records. We shall return the book to the Public Library for him."

"You've been to school," I said, because I was so angry and hungry, and then left the hospital and began walking home.

*   *   *

When I got there I found the street full of automobiles. The house was full of uncles and aunts and cousins from all over the city.

My uncle Khosrove was the first to see me, for he was sitting alone on the steps of the back porch smoking a cigarette.

He got up and shouted at the top of his voice into the house, "I told you it was a mistake. Here he is now, the same as ever, but very much in need of food."

Everybody inside the house came tumbling out, and then, after having seen me, they all hurried back in to set the table.

After I had had all the food I could get into my belly, my mother asked very sweetly, "Why did they come in an ambulance and say that you had died?"

"If I had known they were going to come in an ambulance," I said, "I would have come with them instead of walking three miles on an empty stomach at ten o'clock at night. They didn't tell me they were going to come in an ambulance."

"We've been terribly worried about you," my uncle Zorab said.

This was too much for my uncle Khosrove.

"We've been terribly worried about you!" he mocked. "When the man from the County Hospital told us you were dead, we were afraid you would not recover."

He turned to my uncle Zorab.

"Why do you talk nonsense?" he said. "Is it possible to worry about someone who is dead?"

My uncle Zorab cleared his throat nervously as he said, "Well, all I can say is, we worried, and here he is alive!"

"Man," my uncle Khosrove shouted, "will you never understand the very simplest sort of thing? There has been a mistake, as I said. Your worrying did not bring a dead man back to life. The boy's been involved in some sort of typical American complication. Unless you understand this now, there is no telling what terrible distortions will come into the telling of this family episode in years to come. Now that the boy has had his supper, let him tell us the whole story, and then one by one let us return to our own homes and our own lives. Whoever it was that died, we shall all join him soon enough, and it is quite all right. He turned to me. Now tell us what it was that happened which the people of the hospital reported to us as having been your death at the age of twenty-seven. I tried to tell these people that it was not you who had died, for you are not twenty-seven years old, but they replied that perhaps you had given twenty-seven as your age in a last attempt to be impressive. How old are you, and then tell us the story."

"I'm fourteen," I said.

And then I told the whole story, accurately, point by point.

My aunt Khatoon took to weeping softly for the young man who had died, claiming that he had died for *me,* so that I might go on living, a theory that made my mother angry; but my grandfather twisted his moustaches and said, "All very well and good, but who the devil is this man Kierkegaard to make such an ungodly fuss in this desolate and far-away village which is trying to pass for a city?"

"He is the man who wrote one of the three books I borrowed from the Public Library this afternoon, I said, but that's all I know about him."

"Well," my grandfather said, "that's fine. Now, all of you—get out of here. Go home where you belong. If it's for him you've been crying, there he is trying to get meat from between his teeth, so go home."

Everybody embraced lightly by way of celebrating my survival; there was kindly whispering among the women; the small boys took to wrestling in the living-room; and then at last everybody was gone excepting the Old Man and my uncle Khosrove. These two exchanged quarrelsome glances and then my uncle Khosrove said, "I know what you are going to ask him. Well, I'll give you the answer, to save him the trouble. You are going to ask him what he means by getting into complications of all sorts every other Friday, and I will answer for him that he doesn't mean anything at all by it. Some people come into this world asleep and go out of it asleep, and that is very thoughtful of them. A few others—like myself and this boy, my nephew Aram Garoghlanian—come into this world asleep, and then one fair Friday wake up and look around and notice what we are."

"What are we?" the Old Man asked politely.

"Armenians," my uncle Khosrove said quickly. "Could anything be more ridiculous? The Englishman has an empire to govern. The Frenchman has art to guide and measure. The German has an army to train and test. The Russian has a revolution to start. The Swiss have hotels to manage, the Mexicans mandolins to play, the Spaniards bulls to fight, the Austrians waltzes to dance to, and so on and so forth, but what have *we*?"

"Loud mouths to shut up?" the Old Man suggested.

"And the Irish," my uncle Khosrove went on. "The Irish have a whole island in which to be poverty-stricken; the Arabs a thousand tribes to bring together in the desert; the Jews child prodigies to send on concert tours; the Gypsies wagons and fortune-telling cards; the Americans chronic nervousness which they call freedom, but what have the Armenians?"

"Since you insist, tell me," said the Old Man. "What have the Armenians?"

"Manners," my uncle Khosrove said.

"Are you mad?" the Old Man said. "Nothing is so unnatural as a polite Armenian."

"I did not say *good* manners," my uncle Khosrove said. "I said manners. The good or bad of it I leave to others. Manners is what we have, and very little of anything else. You are going to ask this boy what he means by getting into complications of all sorts every other Friday. Your asking is manners. Well, go ahead and ask him. I'm going to the Arax Coffee House for a couple of hours of tavli. My going is more manners."

"Before you go," the Old Man said, "I think you ought to know I wished to ask the boy to report to me about the book by Kierkegaard, if he ever reads it. Now, I will go to the Coffee House *with* you."

The Old Man got up and yawned enormously. He yawned in three movements, after the fashion of symphonies, very slowly, wildly, and finally slowly and wildly by turns.

He went out of the house by the front door while my uncle Khosrove took the back. The screen doors slammed one-two, and I went looking for half a watermelon to eat, as I was very thirsty.

The following day I went out to the County Hospital and after a great deal of effort identified myself, retrieved my book, and took it home to read. The injured man had reached page 99, for he had folded the edge of that page over, so that he might easily find his place when next he took it up. After reading an hour and three-quarters I too reached page 99, and decided that I did not wish to read any farther. I took the book back to the Public Library and as I had expected the girl at the desk noticed the damage, examined it, examined me as I whistled softly, but did not say anything. I climbed the steep stairway to the mezzanine and continued my search for the book of theology that I hoped to find.

That evening I reported to my grandfather that Kierkegaard appeared to have been a Dane who had been born in 1813 and had died in 1855 after having spent the greater part of his time struggling with the devil, the church, and the complications of theology.

"Died at the age of forty-two," the Old Man said. "Struggling with the devil is most destructive, I see, but perhaps had he *not* struggled he would have lived only twenty-two years and left behind him not even the book he wrote. Have you read the book?"

"He wrote more than one book," I said. "I read the first 99 pages of one of them, and then I got tired of it."

"What did he say in the first 99 pages?"

"I'm not sure, but he *seemed* to say that everything is not enough."

"That is how it is with these fellows who are forever struggling with the devil," the Old Man said. "And the unfortunate man you met yesterday in the Santa Fe freight yards, what about him?"

"He died. Yesterday was the end of the world for him all right, just as he said."

"His real name?"

"Well," I said, "I have a name written down here from the book at the County Hospital which is *supposed* to be his name, but I am sure it is only another mistake. It's no mistake that he's dead, though. I suppose he might have lived had he not fallen into the hands of people so sure of themselves, and so quick to get things accurately wrong. I'm sure he didn't expect to die, for he turned down a page of the book, so that he might go on reading it. Here's the name I got from the Hospital book. Abo Mogabgab."

"How can that be?" the Old Man said. "Abo Mogabgab is the man from whom I buy my clothing, the Syrian with the shop on

Mariposa Street, a man older than myself. Here, look into the lining of this coat at the label and read to me what is said there."

I looked at the label inside the coat and read aloud, "Abo Mogabgab."

"A magnificent example of American efficiency and theological accuracy," the Old Man said. "A man has been killed and a coat label has been given a funeral. And yet, here we are, all of us who are still alive, none the worse for the terrible efficiency or the fierce accuracy. Thank you for reporting to me on the gospel of Kierkegaard. I am still eager to learn, but I find that the farmer's gospel is still the best we have. Now, the vine is planted thus; and thus is it tended; and thus protected from rabbits; and thus are the grapes harvested; and thus are they made into wine; and thus dried by the sun into raisins; and in the winter thus it is that the branches of the vines are pruned; and in the spring thus it is that the vines are watered. What other gospel is half so pleasant, since it is all out in the weather? To hell with these stifling chambers in which poor men sit and confuse themselves. When they are all through for the day, don't they get up and go home and eat a bowl of stewed raisins with a piece of black bread, or drink a glass of wine with a lamb-chop, or eat a bunch of grapes with cheese and crackers?"

"I guess so," I said and went home.

When I got there I spent three hours in the backyard, working. My uncle Khosrove sat on the steps of the back porch and watched.

At last he got up and said, "For the love of God, what is it now? Why are you pestering the life out of that poor old Malaga vine? You have cleaned and repaired it until it looks like the ghost of a wretched old man, and only a moment ago it resembled a handsome, dreaming youth. Matter is beautiful only in its imperfections. Only blockheads seek perfection, which is death. Let perfection seek you. You needn't seek it."

Now, go inside the house and sit down and eat half a cold watermelon. You are not perfect, the vine is not perfect, but you can eat watermelon and pass water, so do so."

"What nonsense," I thought, but as I ate the watermelon I wondered if my uncle Khosrove was not just about the best theological student of them all.

Love, Here Is My Hat

When I woke up I didn't know what time it was, what day, or what city. I knew I was in a hotel room. It seemed to be either pretty late or a small town. I didn't know whether to get up or to go on lying on the bed in my clothes. It was dark.

I knew I was feeling the same.

Love is absurd, always has been, always will be. It's the only thing, but it's absurd. It's too good for anything but birds. It's too splendid for any form of life that's cluttered up with all the crazy things the human form of life is cluttered up with. It's too fine for creatures which wear clothes, which inhabit the world, who must work, who must earn money, who cannot live on air and water.

It's too good for animals that can talk.

I woke up and remembered where I was and why. I was in a room in the Riverside Hotel in Reno and I wasn't in Reno for divorce because I wasn't married. I was in Reno because she was in San Francisco.

I'm not a canary, oriole, dove, quail, robin, hummingbird, or any other kind of feathered creature that lives in or near trees, and exists only to love another canary, oriole, dove, quail, robin, or hummingbird, and sing about it. I'm an American. Fun is fun, but I know the difference between good wholesome fun and love, and love is too good for me or anybody like me. It's too wonderful. I can't fly and I can't sing and I need honest-to-God nourishment. I've got to have rare roast beef at least once a day and when I'm in love I can't eat.

I can't be that nice, either, and not feel ridiculous. It isn't my nature to be that nice. That may be all right for an oriole, but it's just a little absurd for me. I can be that nice when I don't mean it, but when I mean it, it's just too wonderful for words. Being that nice is all right for some good-looking dope in a movie, but it's just too wonderful in San Francisco.

I was in Reno because I wanted her to start eating regularly again and let me eat regularly too. I wanted her to get well, so I could get well too.

Look, I told her in San Francisco, I'm getting awfully hungry. Will you excuse me while I leave town?

Leave town? she said. If you go, I go.

Nothing would please me more, I said, but if you go with me, we won't be able to eat and what we need is food. We're both under-nourished. Look at me. I'm scarcely a shadow of what I was three weeks ago.

You look wonderful, she said.

No, I don't, I said. I look hungry. I *am* hungry. You look hungry too.

I don't care if I do, she said. If you go away, I'm going with you. I can't live without you.

Yes, you can, I said. What you can't live without is—roast beef.

I don't care if I ever eat again, she said.

Look, I said. You've got to get some food and sleep, and so do I.

I won't let you go, she said.

All right, I said. Then we'll die of starvation together. It's all right with me if it's all right with you.

It's all right with me, she said.

All right, I said. I won't go. What shall we do? I mean, first?

It was a little after eleven and we had just gotten home after a movie and an attempt to eat sandwiches that wouldn't go down, except dry. We ate the pickles and drank the coffee.

Let's stay here and listen to the phonograph, she said,

Or shall we go out and have a few drinks? I said.

Wouldn't you rather stay here and listen to the phonograph? she said.

I guess I would, I said.

So we went to bed.

It might have been a couple of orioles.

Three days later, though, we decided to let me go away. We laughed and she said she wouldn't try to find out where I had gone to and wouldn't follow me and I said I wouldn't write, wire, or telephone her.

I feel sick, she said.

Don't be silly, I said. Get in bed and go to sleep and when you wake up, have them bring you a big tray of food. Keep that up for a week.

All right, she said.

I rode to the airport in a cab and two hours later I was in Reno. Fifteen minutes later I was asleep in this room in the Riverside Hotel. I slept like a baby and when I woke up I didn't know what time it was, what day, or what city. Little by little I began to remember.

I got up and yawned. Then I went downstairs and ate a hearty but sad supper of rare roast beef. I don't think it did me much good. After supper I took a walk around town. It was bright and pleasant, but I didn't feel right. I wished I was back in San Francisco, so I got into a cab and rode out of town to The Tavern where I had eight or nine drinks. When I got back to the hotel it was a quarter after two. The desk clerk handed me the key to my room and eleven slips of paper asking me to telephone 783-J. That was a local number. I went to my room and telephoned 783-J.

Where are you? I said.

I'm in Reno, she said.

I know, I said. But where?

I'm at Leon & Eddy's, she said. That number's the number of the phone in the booth here. I'm drunk.

I'll come and get you, I said.

Are you all right? she said.

I'm fine, I said. Are you all right?

I want to cry, she said.

I'll come and get you, I said.

Did you eat? she said.

Yes, I said. Did you?

No, she said. I couldn't.

I'll be right down. How did you know I was in Reno?

The desk clerk told me, she said. I asked him if he knew where you had gone and he told me you had gone to Reno. He told the name of the hotel too. Did you tell him?

Yes, I said.

I didn't think you would, she said. Why did you do it?

I don't know, I said. I guess I thought maybe you might ask him. Why did you ask him?

I thought maybe you might tell him, she said.

I'll be right down, I said.

Leon & Eddy's was two blocks from the hotel, but I took a cab anyway.

When I saw her sitting at the small table, holding the tall glass and looking alone and lonely, I felt sick and happy again, only worse. It was goofy. It was the only thing, but it was crazy.

Come on, I said.

It was too good for me or anybody like me, but it seemed to be the will of the good Lord.

We walked to the hotel.

What we'll have to do, I said, is quarrel and hate one another. It's no use getting married.

I won't quarrel, she said.

We're bound to find something to quarrel about, I said. It may take another day or two, but we're bound to find something. If we don't, it'll be just too bad. This is terrible. I love you.

I love you too, she said.

We stayed in Reno eleven days. Then I told her what I knew she knew I was going to tell her.

Everything's fine, I said. I want it to stay that way.

All right, she said. But we didn't quarrel, did we?

No, I said. Would you prefer a small quarrel?

No, she said.

I'm glad we met, I said.

I took a train back to Frisco and was sick all the way. I knew I would get well, though, and I did.

It took me a long time, but after I got well, nothing was spoiled, and the next time I saw her, three months later, she was well too, so we had supper together.

It was the biggest and finest supper we ever had together, and we enjoyed everything.

Isn't it wonderful? she said.

It certainly is, I said.

from *The Bicycle Rider in Beverly Hills*

I have driven my Cadillac more than 100,000 miles. The cross-country drives were great, from the Pacific to the Atlantic, or the other way around. But I have never driven to evening without loneliness, despair, regret, and all the other things that are of the end. For one end evokes the others, and the end of day evokes the end of life, especially for the traveler. The end of life evokes the errors of it, and a fellow wishes he had known better.

I almost always drove alone. That is the privilege of the traveler who goes by car. Certain drives are like an affair, and they have got to be private. A man is in love with a great many things strewn about haphazardly all over the country. He gets in his car and drives out to them, to have another look at them, and he doesn't want anybody to be sitting beside him. A man can be in love with streets, towns, and cities: railroad tracks, telegraph poles, houses, porches, lawns. He can go out in search of a fresh assorting and arranging of these things, and of the people of them.

A man's car can thus become a pew on wheels—in the church of the world. That is why I have always been angry when my car has failed to work as I have expected it to work, for this has been a failure of my own soul in search of truth. I could have searched in any case, but the automobile gave breadth and depth to the search. The truth is not in the landscape, but neither is it out of it. My car is not like any other car in the world. It is my car and it is like myself.

Before I was sixteen I had many bicycles. I have no idea what became of them. I remember, though, that I rode them so hard they were always breaking down. The spokes of the wheels were always getting loose so that the wheels became crooked. The chains were always breaking. I bore down on the handlebars with so much force in sprinting, in speeding, in making quick getaways, that the handlebars were always getting loose and I was always tightening them. But the thing about my bicycles that I want to remember is the way I rode them, what I thought while I rode them, and the music that came to me.

First of all, my bikes were always rebuilt second-hand bikes. They were lean, hard, tough, swift, and designed for usage. I rode them with speed and style. I found out a great deal about style from riding them. Style in writing, I mean. Style in everything. I did not ride for pleasure. I rode to get somewhere, and I don't mean from the house on San Benito Avenue in Fresno to the Public Library there. I mean I rode to get somewhere *myself*. I did not loaf on my bike. I sometimes rested on it after a hard day's riding, on my way home to supper and sleep, sliding off the seat a little to the left, pedaling with the left leg, resting the other on the saddle, and letting the bike weave right and left easily as I moved forward. The style I learned was this: I learned to go and make it fast. I learned to know at one and the same time how my bike was going, how it was holding up, where I was, where I would soon be, and where in all probability I would finally be.

In the end I always went home to supper and sleep.

A man learns style from everything, but I learned mine from things on which I moved, and as writing is a thing which moves I think I was lucky to learn as I did.

A bike can be an important appurtenance of an important ritual. Moving the legs evenly and steadily soon brings home to the bike-rider a valuable knowledge of pace and rhythm, and a sensible respect for timing and the meeting of a schedule.

Out of rhythm come many things, perhaps all things. The physical action compels action of another order—action of mind, memory, imagination, dream, hope, order, and so on. The physical action also establishes a deep respect for grace, seemliness, effectiveness, power with ease, naturalness, and so on. The action of the imagination brings home to the bicycle-rider the limitlessness of the potential in all things. He finds out that there are many excellent ways in which to ride a bike effectively, and this acquaintanceship with the ways and the comparing of them gives him an awareness of a parallel potential in all other actions. Out of the imagination comes also music and memory.

In the early days of the search I heard many great symphonies which no composer ever put to paper and no orchestra ever performed. This is understandable, I hope. As the saying is, they came to me. I was born restless and was forever eager to be going. There never seemed to be enough of going for me. I wanted to get out to more and more. This might have worn me out, but what it actually did was refresh and strengthen me. Wanting to go and not being able to do so might have given me another order of strength, but the order that I received was to *want* to go and to go. To want to search and to do so.

On the way I found out all the things without which I could never be the writer I am. I was not yet sixteen when I understood a great deal, from having ridden bicycles for so long, about style, speed, grace, purpose, value, form, integrity, health, humor, music, breathing, and finally and perhaps best of all the relationship between the beginning and the end.

My eyes (by which I lived even more than by bread, by which, that is, living had reason, purpose, and a hope of meaning) were continuously assaulted by the elements, especially during the three years I rode a bicycle for a living. Unless I was able to see clearly my entire efficiency as a bicycle-rider was nullified, and I found myself at the side of the road, the bike halted but still propped up under me while I tried to restore vision to my eyes.

The wind carried many things into my eyes, and these things did everything from blur my vision to stop it entirely. The things were dust, dirt, pieces of fine gravel, insects, soot, cinders, and many other things. These things were lifted off the ground or driven out of the air into my eyes. I was forever in trouble with the wind. Insects stang in my eyes, filling them with the water which meant to cleanse them. After they were cleansed it would be some time before the eyes were restored to clear vision. Dirt—anything—in my eyes always brought me to an instantaneous halt, and I didn't like to halt. I once bought a pair of inexpensive goggles and wore them, but they were no good at all. The goggles bothered my eyes. I put them away, and thereafter the way it worked was this: I hoped not to have the wind blow anything into my eyes. But I doubt if there ever was a whole day in which nothing was blown into them.

I loved the wind, but it was often a great nuisance to me, a maker of bitter mischief. More than anything else I needed to see clearly. That was what it came to. In order to go—which was my work—I had to be able to see where I was going. Not to see where I was going meant that I had to stop. And to stop was to fail. And I did not enjoy failing. I have always been angered by failure. I am still angered by it. My success as a telegraph messenger depended on my eyes. Consequently, *all* hope of effectiveness depended on them. My effectiveness as a messenger became inseparable from my hope to be effective as a writer.

There were times when blindness, despair, and anger were so great that I believed I would throw it all over, turn in my messenger's coat and cap, put aside my bike, keep myself and my eyes out of the wind, sit down in the Public Library, and devote my time exclusively to the book, my eyes entirely secure now from the wind. But that was not to be.

First I needed the money the job brought me. That is, the Saroyan family needed it.

Second, I needed the action of myself in the world. That is, the writer needed it.

Third, I needed to go, to continue to go, to continue my study of rhythm, pace, speed, and effectiveness. I needed all this in order to understand who I was, who I could be, and how.

Watching the wind work far off on eucalyptus trees was a great joy. Listening to it among the leaves of them when I reached the trees was sweet music. But best of all was when the wind had great power, when it was erratic and did swift and sudden things, stopped suddenly, picked up suddenly, ran in a circle, sprinted straight ahead, stopped, turned, came back.

Now and then when the wind was very strong I found it difficult to make my way through it on my bike, but I don't believe it was ever able to stop me entirely, except through trickery, by blinding me with dirt. Many times it almost unseated me, but I always managed to hang on.

The wind with the rain made other difficulties. Getting wet meant little or nothing, but rain driven into the eyes by the wind can also blur the vision. The difficulty of blurred vision is great, almost greater than blindness itself, for the eye with blurred vision likes to believe it still has enough vision on which to keep going. I soon learned, however, that to keep going when vision is poor is folly. Even so, I was often tempted to take a chance. If I had no work to do the wind and the rain would have been a joy to behold. The weather fascinated me, especially storms, but it is one thing to watch a storm and another to fight it.

A second difficulty for the bike-rider in the rain is the slipperiness of the streets and the muddiness of the roads. I have had to get off my bike on muddy roads and push through on foot to where I was to deliver a telegram. Many times I slipped and spilled on the wet streets, for having misjudged the pace I could maintain efficiently.

I also had to be concerned about the vision of others in the streets, the drivers of automobiles especially, for it was not enough for me to see and know where I was going, it was necessary to see where a motorist was going, and be able to predict where he would soon be.

The heat of the summer softened the tar of the outlying streets of Fresno, so that getting the bike over them meant rising up off the saddle and bringing the entire weight of the body to bear upon the pedals—or sprinting, although the amount of speed I was able to achieve may scarcely be associated with the implication of the word sprint. More often than not I was barely able to keep the bike from stopping, but that was the idea—to *move* myself upon my bike to where I was going.

The heat and the riding in it all day made me very thirsty. This thirst was almost unquenchable during July, August, and September. I had a lot of respect for money, consequently I was not given to throwing it around on treats for myself, but after a great deal of thought I saw the wisdom of one transaction that I made at least once a day in the summer, occasionally twice a day. There was a place named The Danish Dairy on Fresno Avenue, across the street from the Hippodrome Theater, where for five cents anybody could stand and pour cold buttermilk out of a pitcher into a tall glass and drink as much as he liked. This was the perfect drink for the messenger in the summer. Around two or half past two in the afternoon when I stepped into The Danish Dairy I would drink a great deal of buttermilk for five cents. I never drank fewer than four large glasses of it, and frequently, taking my time on the last two or three glasses, I drank seven or eight. The liquid was especially thirst-quenching, cooling, and deeply satisfying. It was also food. The girls and women who took care of the buttermilk-drinkers knew me well and did not ever suggest by any act of expression that I was going too far. If anything they seemed pleased to see me and glad when I drank a very great deal of buttermilk. The little specks of butter floating on top or swimming throughout the liquid were a delight when they were filtered in the mouth and tasted. The big salt-shaker was there on the white marble counter—half a dozen of them—and the taste of the salt was a real joy. The place smelled clean and wonderful, it was cool, and the faces and bodies of the girls and women were fresh and sweet-smelling. The drinking of the buttermilk every afternoon was something I looked forward to all day, and the actual drinking of it was something that made me feel absolutely lordly in my aliveness.

The work was hard, but The Danish Dairy was there, and for a nickel I could drink all the cold buttermilk I liked. And I did. That was one of the great pleasures of the summer, almost as good as the eating of cold watermelon at home after work. I frequently ate an entire watermelon, and not a small one. The summer brought deep thirst to me, and there were good things by which to quench it.

My ears (by which, with my eyes, I lived and learned) had excellent hearing until I was seventeen or eighteen, so that I heard the sounds made by very small creatures, all manner of insects, mice at night, hummingbirds, leaves stirring or letting go and falling, soft whistlings, hummings, moanings.

When I was surely not much more than six, though, I began to hear with the inner ear, too, and although my memory is inaccurate about some of this I know that one of the important inner sounds I heard was what I must call the sound of wings.

This was probably the result of nothing more than an actual apparatus of the interior ear adjusting itself, restoring itself, fighting off illness or partial deafness, or the action of blood itself in my head at a moment of partial blockade somewhere, in some small but important vein in some small but important area. Or it was something else, something I have no way of naming. Whatever it was, from time to time, and not always at night before I fell asleep, I would hear (and feel) a plunging, shifting, charging action in my head which seemed to me to have a quality of swift flight, as if an enormous wing had brushed my soul. When this action was first noticed by me it stopped me cold on my tracks and frightened me, for I felt that the wing was death. A small boy is apt to give an experience of this order such a value. Later on, much later on, the action having become familiar was considered nothing, certainly nothing stranger than the continuous accumulation of phlegm in my nasal passages and throat.

I heard other things with the inner ear. I have already mentioned the music I heard. I had better remark further on this. As I rode my bike, music began to *happen* to me. Insofar as I am able to describe it it was orchestral music. The piano was often involved, but on the whole the music was that of a large orchestra which had become a single instrument. The music had magnificent form, great accumulative power, and passion of a high order—the passion, that is, of control, restraint, and denial—the human conditions out of which we know collective passion is most apt to reach an individual body and soul. Even though I alone knew about this music, I cherished it deeply and took great pride in it.

I both listened to the music and made it, or at any rate so it seemed. It was certainly happening to me, and it was happening as I performed other, less magnificent, work—as I delivered or picked up telegrams. The adventure of the music was always great, but in a quiet way. While the music was happening I kept wondering how it would fulfill itself, how it would round out its form and be finished. The music, I think it is quite understandable, tended to end when a bike ride ended, but this was not always so. Frequently one work, in one key of music or one dimension of memory or inner experience, would endure an entire work day and then carry itself over into evening, night, and sleep. In the morning, though, it would be gone and forgotten. It would be forgotten, that is, in its details, but not in its quality. If I took to the music actively and began to whistle as well as listen to it, this did not stop the orchestra. But when the bike ride ended and it was time for me to go among people to deliver or pick up a telegram, the orchestral portion of the music would fall away from inner hearing, no doubt because now the external hearing was involved with other sounds, but the whistling would continue while I was among the people, in a business office, or in a grape packing house, or in the telegraph office itself. This whistling bothered some people. The wife of the manager of the telegraph office once complained about it to her husband who took me aside and with some awkwardness asked me not to whistle while I was in the telegraph office. I was astonished by this request for two reasons: first, because I hadn't been aware of the whistling, and second, because I couldn't imagine anybody resenting it. But genius is often deeply resented by small souls, so that if the world were a reasonable place all geniuses would be despised outcasts and eccentrics.

I was not always lucky in what I heard. It was not always an orchestra at work on a grand symphony. It was frequently a song, and quite strangely it would be a song which was not whole, which never in fact became whole. It would be a fragment of a song, certainly insofar as the words were concerned. And here perhaps lies the clue to the failure of this form to fulfill itself—its involvement in words. For words are inadequate instruments of communication, or of the making of wholeness. Sounds and rhythms and measures must apparently see themselves through to ends, but words must be *driven* to their ends, and that is the difficulty and majesty of writing. All the same I was lucky enough. At a time when the air of the world still had purity I heard great music which no one else heard.

I was thirteen when I bought a phonograph and one record and carried it home under my arm on my bicycle to the house on San Benito Avenue. My mother was fiercely angry at me for spending twelve dollars on a piece of junk. She cursed the machine and me and was unable not to come at me with such violence that I had to run out of the house. She followed me in a kind of insane but nevertheless comic chase around the house. The phonograph was resting on the table in the parlor. I ran quickly up the front porch steps, into the parlor to the phonograph. I quickly wound it, put needle to disc, and ran out of the house again just as my mother came into the parlor. She was on her way after me when she began to hear the music of the phonograph record. It was something called *Sonia*, performed by Paul Whiteman's band. I expected my mother to continue the chase, but she didn't. I myself stopped in the backyard to listen to the music. After about a minute I went back into the house. My mother was standing over the machine, listening to the music. Her anger was gone and in place of it I saw in her face the deep sorrow of her nature, her family, her race. A moment of jazz-band orchestration had done this.

When the record ended she turned to me and said, "All right. I had no idea. It is all right. Take good care of the machine. You have this one record only?"

I told her there was another song on the reverse side of the record. She sat down and said, "Please let me hear it."

On the reverse side was something called *"Hi-li, Hi-lo,"* I believe.

That was the beginning of external music in my own life, in my own family, and in my own house. My sisters and my brothers were thrilled by the phonograph, and the one record. My mother established the rule that I alone might buy one new record a week, which I did. She waited eagerly for the arrival of this record and she listened to it again and again. This music must have been very strange to her, certainly music altogether unlike anything she had ever heard in Armenia, unlike the hymns she'd heard and sung at church. And yet she loved the music.

After a time I sent two dollars to a mail order house and received twelve records. This was a great bargain. The quality of the music was poor, but having twelve records for the price of three was exciting, and it satisfied the family necessity to be economical in all things.

But I had been listening to my own bike-riding music long before the arrival of the phonograph.

Now, it is important to understand two things: first, that after the phonograph became an important part of the family life I continued to hear my own music, and second, as I listened more and more to the music of the phonograph I heard my own music less and less.

If the external ear is surfeited with music, the internal ear tends to become deaf. If the body is satisfied, the soul tends to become unwilling or unable to seek satisfaction.

A Writer's Declaration

On October 15, 1934, my first book, *The Daring Young Man on the Flying Trapeze and Other Stories,* was published. The year 1934 seems quite near, but the fact remains that it was twenty years ago, as I write. Many things happened in those twenty years, several of them to me.

I didn't earn one dollar by any means other than writing. I wrote short stories, plays, novels, essays, poems, book reviews, miscellaneous comment, letters to editors, private letters, and songs.

Nothing that I wrote was written to order, on assignment, or for money, although a good deal of what I wrote happened to earn money. If an editor liked a story as I had written it, he could buy it. If he wanted parts of it written over, I did not do that work. Nobody did it. One editor took liberties with a short piece about Christmas, and the writer of a cookbook to which I had written a free Preface added a few lines by way of making me out a soldier-patriot. I protested to the editor and to the writer of the cookbook, but of course the damage had been done. During the Second World War I wrote no propaganda of any kind, although I was invited several times to do so. The point is that for twenty years I have been an American writer who has been entirely free and independent.

I consider the past twenty years the first half of my life as a published writer, and the next twenty I consider the second half. At that time I shall be sixty-six years old, which can be very old, or not. I expect to be more creative in the next twenty years than I was in the first twenty, even though I start with a number of handicaps. To begin with, I owe so much in back taxes that it is very nearly impossible arithmetically to even the score by writing, and I have acquired other personal, moral, and financial responsibilities.

I have never been subsidized, I have never accepted money con-
nected with a literary prize or award, I have never been endowed,
and I have never received a grant or fellowship. A year or two after
my first book was published I was urged by friends to file an application for a Guggenheim Fellowship. Against my better judgment I
filed an application, which was necessarily if not deliberately hap-
hazard. How should I know what I wanted to write, for instance? I
couldn't possibly describe it. My application was turned down and
I began to breathe freely again.

I am head over heels in debt. I expect to get out of debt by writing, or not at all. I have no savings account, no stocks or bonds, no
real estate, no insurance, no cash, and no real property that is con-
vertible into anything like a sum of money that might be useful. I
simply have got to hustle for a living. I mention these matters
impersonally, as facts, and not to arouse sympathy. I don't want any.

Had my nature been practical I might at this time know financial security, as it's called. There is nothing wrong with such security, I suppose, but I prefer another kind. I prefer to recognize the
truth that I *must* work, and to believe that I *can*.

I squandered a great deal of money that I earned as a writer and
I lost a lot of it gambling. It seems to have been my nature to squander
and to gamble, that's all. I gave some away, perhaps a great deal. I am
not unaware of the possible meaning of the discomfort I have felt
when I have had money, and the compulsion I have had to get rid
of it somehow or other. I think I have felt the need to be only a
writer, a writing writer, and not a success of any kind.

The ability or compulsion to hoard money has always seemed to
me a complicated if not offensive thing. And yet I have always had
sympathy for those who have been experts at hoarding, at legal
means by which not to pay taxes, at timely thrusts into new and
profitable areas of money-making, such as investments, real estate,
inventions, oil, uranium, government contracts, the backing of
plays, manufacturing, and marketing. The noticeable shrewdness of
such people has always amused me, even when I myself have been
the party to be outwitted.

When I was in the Army, for instance, in the snow of Ohio, in the
dead of winter, a very capable money-man who was quite rich and

young and not in the Army flew from New York to Ohio to discuss with me changes he felt I ought to make in one of my plays on which he had paid me a thousand dollars in advance. I met him whenever the Army regulations permitted me to, and I heard him out, which took a great deal of time I would have preferred to keep to myself. The man talked around and around, and it suddenly occurred to me that what he was really trying to say but couldn't was that he didn't feel the play would be a hit, and that he was help-less not to do something about the thousand dollars. This did not astonish me. I took a check for a thousand dollars to his hotel and left it at the desk, along with a short note. I wanted to see if my hunch was right. It was. We were supposed to meet the following night. We didn't. He flew back to New York with the check, cashed it, and I never heard from him again. There was no legal, or even moral, reason for me to return the thousand dollars. I simply couldn't bear to see him so upset about the small sum of money, all the while pretending that he was concerned only about art.

At one of the biggest moving-picture factories in Hollywood, when I discovered that I had been hoodwinked into making a poor deal, I met the executives who had done the brilliant hoodwinking, I established that they *had* done it, and I got into my car and drove to San Francisco. I was informed several years later that I had left behind wages due me under the terms of the hoodwinking agree-ment that amounted to something between five and fifteen thou-sand dollars. I never investigated the matter. The factory and its chief beneficiaries were hoarding profits by the millions, working diligently and profitably with the government on shabby propa-ganda films, and yet six or seven of the executives found it absolutely necessary to act in unison and to outwit the writer of a story they wanted desperately, from which they acquired three or four more millions of dollars. I have no idea what they have done with their money, but I am sure it has been something cautious and useless.

Before my first book was published I was not a drinker, but soon after it came out I discovered the wisdom of drinking, and I think this is something worth looking into for a moment.

In 1935 I drank moderately, and traveled to Europe for the first time, but the following nine years, until I was drafted into the

Army, I drank as much as I liked, and I frequently drank steadily for nine or ten hours at a time.

I was seldom drunk, however. I enjoyed the fun of drinking and talking loudly with friends—writers, painters, sculptors, newspapermen, and the girls and women we knew in San Francisco.

Drinking with good companions can be a good thing for a writer, but let a writer heed this humble and perhaps unnecessary warning: stop drinking when drinking tends to be an end in itself, for that is a useless end. I believe I have learned a lot while I have been drinking with friends, just as most of us may say we have learned a lot in sleep. There is, however, a recognizable limit to what may be learned by means of drinking.

In the writing that I have done during the past twenty years, what do I regret?

Nothing. Not one word.

Did I write enough?

No. No writer ever writes enough.

Might I have written differently? More intelligently, for instance?

No.

First, I always tried my best, as I understand trying. Second, I believe I was quite intelligent all the time.

Then, what about the theory of certain critics and readers that my writing is unrealistic and sentimental?

Well, I think they are mistaken. In writing that is *effective* I don't think *anything* is unrealistic. As for my own writing, I think it has always been profoundly realistic if not ever superficially so. I don't think my writing is sentimental either, although it is a very sentimental thing to be a human being.

As I write, I am back in San Francisco, where I lived when my first book was published, where I have not lived in six or seven years, and the day is the thirteenth of October. I drove up from Malibu two days ago for a visit of ten or eleven days while my house on the beach is being painted inside and out. I did not drive to San Francisco in order to be here on the twentieth anniversary of the publication of my first book, but I shall be here on that day nevertheless.

Already I have walked in the various neighborhoods of San Francisco I have known, to notice again the various houses in which I have lived: 348 Carl Street, 1707 Divisadero, 2378 Sutter, 123 Natoma: and the various places in which I worked before I had had a story published in a national magazine: various branch offices of the Postal Telegraph Company—on Market Street in the Palace Hotel Building, on Powell Street at Market, on Taylor at Market in the Golden Gate Theatre Building, and at 405 Brannan, near Third.

I was a clerk and teletype operator in the first three offices, but I was the manager of the office on Brannan. I have always been a little proud of that, for I was the youngest manager of a Postal Telegraph branch office in America, nineteen years old and without a high school diploma.

Yesterday I walked through the Crystal Palace Market and visited the stand at which I once hustled potatoes and tomatoes, the *Fiore d'Italia*.

I went into the building at Market and Sixth where the offices of the Cypress Lawn Cemetery Company are located. I worked there, too.

The vice-president said, "Do you intend to make Cypress Lawn your lifetime career?"

I said, "Yes, sir."

I got the job.

I quit a month later, but working there was a valuable experience. I remember the arrival of Christmas week and the vice-president's bitter complaint that owing to the absence of an epidemic of influenza the company's volume of business for December over the previous year had fallen twenty-two per cent.

I remarked, "But everybody will catch up eventually, won't they?"

The vice-president lifted his glasses from the bridge of his nose to his forehead in order to have another look at me.

"I'm a writer," I said. "Unpublished."

He asked me to look at some slogans he had composed for the company: *Inter here. A lot for your money.*

I said he had a flair.

I walked along the Embarcadero to the Dodd Warehouse, across from Pier 17, for I worked there a month, too. The trouble with that job was the floating crap games of the longshoremen every lunch hour in empty boxcars or behind piles of lumber on the docks. My take-home pay every week was nothing, although I made a friend of the great Negro crapshooter and game manager who was called Doughbelly. The sunlight down there on the waterfront during those lunch-hour crap games was wonderful, and as I walked there yesterday I could almost see the huge old man calling the points of the game, and I had to remember that whenever he noticed I wasn't betting he correctly surmised that I was fresh out of funds and slipped me a silver dollar or two so that I might get back into the action.

Once, when I stayed away from the games for three days running in the hope of having a few dollars in my pocket for Saturday night, Doughbelly kept asking everybody, "Where's that Abyssinian boy?"

I was in the Dodd Warehouse eating sandwiches and reading Jack London, that's where I was.

It was at 348 Carl Street twenty years ago on this day, October 13, that I opened a package from Random House and saw a copy of my first book. That was a hell of a moment. I was so excited I couldn't roll a Bull Durham cigarette. After three tries I finally made it, and began to inhale and exhale a little madly as I examined the preposterous and very nearly unbelievable object of art and merchandise. What a book, what a cover, what a title page, what words, what a photograph—now just watch the women swarm around. For a young writer does write in order to expect pretty women to swarm around.

Alas, the swarmers aren't often pretty. This is a mystery that continues to baffle me. Pretty women swarm around fat little men who own and operate small businesses. They swarm around chiropractors who are full of talk about some of their interesting cases and achievements. They swarm around young men who wear black shirts and have five buttons on the sleeves of their sport coats, who have no visible means of support, who spend hours chatting amiably about last night's preposterous trivia as if it were history.

Pretty women swarm around everybody but writers.

Plain, intelligent women *somewhat* swarm around writers.

But it wasn't only to have pretty women swarm around that I hustled my first book into print. It wasn't that alone by a long shot.

I also meant to revolutionize American writing.

In the early thirties the word revolutionize enjoyed popularity and was altogether respectable, but a special poll invented by a special statistician would be the only means today by which to measure my success in revolutionizing American writing. To pretend that my writing hasn't had any effect at all on American writing, however, would be inaccurate. The trouble is that for the most part my writing influenced unpublished writers who remained unpublished, and to measure that kind of an influence calls for a lot of imagination and daring. The good writers that my writing influenced were already published, some of them long published, but the truth is that my writing *did* influence their writing, too, for I began to notice the improvement almost immediately. And I didn't notice it in short stories alone, I noticed it in novels and plays, and even in movies.

What did my writing have that might be useful to writing in general?

Freedom.

I think I demonstrated that if you have a writer, you have writing, and that the writer himself is of greater importance than his writing until he quits, or is dead.

Thus, if you are a writer, you do not have to kill yourself every time you write a story, a play, or a novel.

But why did I want to revolutionize American writing?

I had to, because I didn't like it, and wanted to.

And why, as a writer, was I unwilling to act solemn? Didn't I know that unless I acted solemn the big critics would be afraid to write about my writing? I knew. I refused to act solemn because I didn't feel solemn. I didn't feel I *ought* to feel solemn, or even dignified, because I knew acting dignified was only a shadow removed from being pompous. Some writers are naturally solemn, dignified, or pompous, but that doesn't mean that they are also naturally great, or even effective.

There simply isn't any mysterious connection between solemnity and great writing. Some great writers had great solemnity, but most of them had almost none. They had something else.

What is this other thing?

I think it is an obsession to get to the probable truth about man, nature, and art, straight through everything to the very core of *one's own* being.

What is this probable truth?

It changes from day to day, certainly from year to year. You can measure the change from decade to decade, and the reason you can measure it is that there have been writers (and others) who have been obsessed about it, too.

To become free is the compulsion of our time—free of everything that is useless and false, however deeply established in man's fable. But this hope of freedom, this need of it, does not for a moment mean that man is to go berserk. Quite the contrary, since freedom, real freedom, true freedom, carries the life and fable of man nearer and nearer to order, beauty, grace, and meaning—all of which must always remain correctable in details—revised, improved, refined, enlarged, extended.

Intelligence *is* arriving into the fable of the life of man. It isn't necessarily welcome, though, certainly not in most quarters. In order to be a little less unwelcome it must be joined by humor, out of which the temporary best has always come. You simply cannot call the human race a dirty name unless you smile when you do so. The calling of the name may be necessary and the name itself may be temporarily accurate, but not to smile at the time is a blunder that nullifies usefulness, for without humor there is no hope, and man could no more live without hope than he could without the earth underfoot.

Life rules the world, impersonal and free life. The anonymous living tell their story every day, with the help of professional or amateur writers, but the greatest story-teller of all is time and change, or death. But death is not our doom and not our enemy. Next to birth it is our best gift, and next to truth it is our best friend.

I am back in San Francisco on the occasion of the twentieth anniversary of the publication of my first book—the beginning of my life as a writer, as a force in the life of my time, as a voting representative of my anonymous self and of any and all others whose aspirations parallel my own—to live creatively, to live honorably, to hurt no one insofar as possible, to enjoy mortality, to fear neither death nor immortality, to cherish fools and failures even more than wise men and saints since there are more of them, to believe, to hope, to work, and to do these things with humor.

To say yes, and not to say no.

What advice have I for the potential writer?

I have none, for anybody is a potential writer, and the writer who is a writer needs no advice and seeks none.

What about courses in writing in colleges and universities?

Useless, they are entirely useless.

The writer is a spiritual anarchist as in the depth of his soul every man is. He is discontented with everything and everybody. The writer is everybody's best friend and only true enemy—the good and great enemy. He neither walks with the multitude nor cheers with them. The writer who is a writer is a rebel who never stops. He does not conform for the simple reason that there is nothing yet worth conforming to. When there is something half worth conforming to he will not conform to that, either, or half conform to it. He won't even rest or sleep as other people rest and sleep. When he's dead he'll probably be dead as others are dead, but while he is alive he is alive as no one else is, not even another writer. The writer who is a writer is also a fool. He is the easiest man in the world to belittle, ridicule, dismiss, and scorn: and that also is precisely as it should be. He is also mad, measurably so, but saner than all others, with the best sanity, the only sanity worth bothering about—the living, creative, vulnerable, valorous, unintimidated, and arrogant sanity of a free man.

I am a writer who is a writer, as I have been for twenty years, and expect to be for twenty more.

I am here to stay, and so is everybody else. No explosive is going to be employed by anybody on anybody. Knowing this, believing this, the writer who is a writer makes plans to watch his health casually, and to write his writing with more and more purposeful intelligence, humor, and love.

I am proud of my twenty years, undecorated as they may be. I am proud to be a writer, the writer I am, and I don't care what anybody else is proud of.

Major Works by William Saroyan

The Daring Young Man on the Flying Trapeze and Other Stories
Inhale and Exhale
Three Times Three
My Name Is Aram
The Human Comedy
The Adventures of Wesley Jackson
The Bicycle Rider in Beverly Hills
Here Comes, There Goes, You Know Who
Not Dying
Days of Life and Death and Escape to the Moon
Obituaries
Births

About the Editor

William Emery Justice, a fourth-generation Kansan, attended the University of Kansas, where he studied Russian literature and language, German literature, and religion. He worked as a farm laborer, a pizza maker, a vacuum salesman (he didn't sell a single machine), a roofer, a doughnut fryer, a bookbinder, a convenience store clerk (third shift), a copyist, and a video store clerk before joining Heyday Books. He co-edited *California Uncovered: Stories for the 21st Century* (also published by Heyday Books) and is writing a novel placing Orpheus in a mythical Kansas.

A California Legacy Book

Santa Clara University and Heyday Books are pleased to publish the California Legacy series, vibrant and relevant writings drawn from California's past and present.

Santa Clara University—founded in 1851 on the site of the eighth of California's original twenty-one missions—is the oldest institution of higher learning in the state. A Jesuit institution, it is particularly aware of its contribution to California's cultural heritage and its responsibility to preserve and celebrate that heritage.

Heyday Books, founded in 1974, specializes in critically acclaimed books on California literature, history, natural history, and ethnic studies.

Books in the California Legacy series appear as anthologies, single author collections, reprints of important books, and original works. Taken together, these volumes bring readers a new perspective on California's cultural life, a perspective that honors diversity and finds great pleasure in the eloquence of human expression.

SERIES EDITOR: Terry Beers

PUBLISHER: Malcolm Margolin

ADVISORY COMMITTEE: Stephen Becker, William Deverell, Charles Faulhaber, David Fine, Steven Gilbar, Ron Hansen, Gerald Haslam, Robert Hass, Jack Hicks, Timothy Hodson, James Houston, Jeanne Wakatsuki Houston, Maxine Hong Kingston, Frank LaPena, Ursula K. Le Guin, Jeff Lustig, Tillie Olsen, Ishmael Reed, Alan Rosenus, Robert Senkewicz, Gary Snyder, Kevin Starr, Richard Walker, Alice Waters, Jennifer Watts, Al Young.

Thanks to the English Department at Santa Clara University and to Regis McKenna for their support of the California Legacy series.

Related California Legacy Books

Tales of the Fish Patrol *Jack London*

The Land of Orange Groves and Jails: Upton Sinclair's California
Edited by Lauren Coodley

Merton of the Movies *Harry Leon Wilson*

Gunfight at Mussel Slough: Evolution of a Western Myth
Edited by Terry Beers

California Poetry: From the Gold Rush to the Present
Edited by Dana Gioia, Chryss Yost, and Jack Hicks

Mark Twain's San Francisco
Edited with a New Introduction by Bernard Taper

Storm *George R. Stewart*

Dark God of Eros: A William Everson Reader
Edited with an Introduction by Albert Gelpi

Under the Fifth Sun: Latino Literature in California
Edited by Rick Heide

November Grass *Judy Van der Veer*

Unfinished Message: Selected Works of Toshio Mori
Introduction by Lawson Fusao Inada

And many others.

For more California Legacy titles, events, or other information, please visit www.californialegacy.org. If you would like to be added to the California Legacy mailing list, please send your name, address, phone number, and email address to:

> California Legacy Project
> English Department
> Santa Clara University
> Santa Clara, CA 95053